Chinese Legal Translation

Chinese Legal Translation analyses and investigates the Chinese translation of conditional clauses introduced by various introductory words in Hong Kong bilingual ordinances within the framework of descriptive translation studies and translation typology.

This book explores the text typology of Hong Kong bilingual ordinances and highlights differences and similarities between different translations of conditional clauses in the Hong Kong context. Based on both quantitative and qualitative analysis of conditional clauses of the Companies Ordinance, the book summarises the frequency of introductory words of conditional clauses and generalises guiding patterns for writing conditional clauses and translating conditional clauses. The book is significant in providing both theoretical foundations for legal translation and practical guidance for translating legal conditional clauses.

This book is primarily targeted at scholars and professionals who are interested in legal writing and legal translation, as well as students and practitioners in legal translation.

Yan Wang is a Lecturer in the Department of Translation at the Chinese University of Hong Kong.

Routledge Studies in Chinese Translation
Series Editor: Chris Shei, Swansea University, UK

This series encompasses scholarly works on every possible translation activity and theory involving the use of Chinese language. Putting together an important knowledge base for Chinese and Westerner researchers on translation studies, the series draws on multiple disciplines for essential information and further research that is based on or relevant to Chinese translation.

Titles include:

Terminology Translation in Chinese Contexts
Theory and Practice
Edited by Saihong Li and William Hope

Mapping the Translator
A Study in Liang Shiqiu
Liping Bai

The Translator's Mirror for the Romantic
Cao Xueqin's *Dream* and David Hawkes' *Stone*
Fan Shengyu

Dialect, Voice, and Identity in Chinese Translation
A Descriptive Study of Chinese Translations of *Huckleberry Finn, Tess*, and *Pygmalion*
Jing Yu

A Deaf Take on Non-Equivalence in Written Chinese Translation
Chan Yi Hin

The Works of Lin Yutang
Translation and Recognition
Yangyang Long

Chinese Legal Translation
An Analysis of Conditional Clauses in Hong Kong Bilingual Ordinances
Yan Wang

For a full list of titles and more information about this series, please visit: https://www.routledge.com/Routledge-Studies-in-Chinese-Translation/book-series/RSCT

Chinese Legal Translation

An Analysis of Conditional Clauses in Hong Kong Bilingual Ordinances

Yan Wang

Routledge
Taylor & Francis Group
LONDON AND NEW YORK

First published 2024
by Routledge
4 Park Square, Milton Park, Abingdon, Oxon OX14 4RN

and by Routledge
605 Third Avenue, New York, NY 10158

Routledge is an imprint of the Taylor & Francis Group, an informa business

British Library Cataloguing-in-Publication Data
A catalogue record for this book is available from the British Library

ISBN: 978-1-032-41670-0 (hbk)
ISBN: 978-1-032-41669-4 (pbk)
ISBN: 978-1-003-35918-0 (ebk)

DOI: 10.4324/9781003359180

Typeset in Times New Roman
by Deanta Global Publishing Services, Chennai, India

For my dear boy Yu Cun

Contents

Tables and Figures

Tables

Figures

Preface

This book discusses the translation of conditional clauses in Hong Kong bilingual ordinances, in an attempt to explore different translations for introductory words of conditional clauses and translation patterns for various types of conditional clauses. To be specific, by analysing and describing conditional clauses and their translations found in the Companies Ordinance of Hong Kong bilingual ordinances, this study investigates different translation approaches for introductory words for conditional clauses, i.e., 'if,' 'where,' 'when,' 'in (the) case,' and 'in the event.' Additionally, the sampling research method is employed to focus on analysing conditional clauses introduced by 'if' and 'where,' in order to identify translation patterns for conditional clauses. This may provide feasible translation patterns for legal translation practitioners in their work when translating conditional clauses—dominant sentence structures in legal texts.

Different scholars vary in their views on the text types of legal texts. Based on the theories of translation typology, the author, after summarising the opinions of multiple scholars on the legal text type, proposes a new viewpoint on the text type of legal texts. Specifically, when the translated text serves the same function as the original text, the function of the legal text is vocative; when the function of the translated text differs from that of the original text, the function of the original legal text is vocative while the function of the translated text can be informative or expressive. Given that bilingual versions of Hong Kong ordinances are authentic and carry the same and equal legal effect, the translated text serves the same function as the original text, so both versions of Hong Kong bilingual ordinances are vocative. Based on this new perspective, the book conducts a detailed analysis of different translations for introductory words of conditional clauses in the Companies Ordinance, so as to examine whether these translations achieve the same function as the original text.

Therefore, within the framework of descriptive translation studies and translation typology, the book analyses and investigates the Chinese translation of conditional clauses introduced by various introductory words in Hong Kong bilingual ordinances, with a view to exploring the text typology of Hong Kong bilingual ordinances, and highlighting differences and similarities between different translations of conditional clauses in the Hong Kong context. Based on both quantitative and qualitative analysis of conditional clauses of the Companies Ordinance, the book summarises the frequency of introductory words of conditional clauses and generalises guiding patterns for writing conditional clauses and translating conditional clauses. Besides, to tackle various conditional clauses, which are complicated and challenging, different analytical methods for the translation of conditional clauses are also presented in the book. The book is significant in providing both theoretical foundations for legal translation and practical guidance for translating legal conditional clauses. This book is primarily targeted at scholars and professionals who are interested in legal writing and legal translation, as well as students and practitioners in legal translation.

This book, based on my MPhil dissertation completed at the Hong Kong Polytechnic University in 2011, is now ready after years of teaching experience in legal translation and months of efforts in revising and polishing. This book would never have been possible without the help of my MPhil supervisors Dr Kexing Li and Prof. Chiyu Chu who led me into translation studies and legal translation years ago. I could never thank them enough for their guidance and patience during my study and post-study trip. My heartfelt gratitude goes to Dr Bo Wang, Dr Chris Shei, the editors at Routledge, Iola Ashby and Andrea Hartill, and my book reviewers. Last but not least, I would like to extend my thanks to my supportive family, my parents, my husband Mr. Dijia Liao, and my son Yucun Liao, for their endless love and understanding.

1 Introduction

Legal writing and legal translation

1.1 Research background

1.1.1 Law and legal language

Law is the highest standard formulated or recognised by the state and enforced by the state apparatus to regulate and constrain the behaviour of society as a whole, with supreme authority and normativity. Therefore, the language used in legal expressions (i.e., legal language) and the compositions formed by legal language (i.e., legal texts) primarily serve the purpose or intention of achieving this regulatory function. Legal texts have a regulatory and constraining function to govern and guide activities and behaviours between individuals and society, and among individuals, in the domains of politics, the economy, and culture, amongst others. The regulatory function of legal texts is protected by the coercive power of the state and possesses enforceability (Li & Zhang, 2005: 10). This is also one of the main factors that differentiate legal texts from other types of texts.

Language is an established system of norms that must be followed by society as a whole. The same applies to legal language. In China, the term used for legal language was initially '法言' (fǎ yán; law language) or '法語' (fǎ yǔ; law language). According to *Ciyuan*, the most authoritative dictionary for checking old Chinese or archaic Chinese, the term '法言' has two meanings: (1) speeches or remarks that comply with Confucian ritual and law; (2) similar to aphorisms. As for '法語,' it shares similar meanings with '法言.' Both refer to normative language with guiding functions that people must comply with.

Cao (2007: 13) identifies the nature of legal language as normative, performative, technical, and indeterminate. Goodrich, an American law professor, deems that 'to learn the law is first and foremost to learn the language of law and the coincident linguistic skills whereby that knowledge can be used in legal practice' (1987: 297). There is a close connection between law and language. According to Gibbons (2003: 1–2), a prominent contemporary legal linguist, 'The law is an overwhelmingly linguistic institution … It is, therefore, not only the law that permeates our lives but the language of the law.' Thus, legal language carries the coercive power of law which in turn features legal language with authority and binding force.

DOI: 10.4324/9781003359180-1

1.1.2 Legal texts

Legal texts, a broad and inclusive concept, include laws, regulations, treaties, international conventions, international customs, foreign economic contracts, and judicial texts, amongst others. According to Wang (2006: 3), the translation of legal texts includes two cases: (1) translation for reference purposes only, such as translating Chinese legal provisions into English for the convenience of non-Chinese speakers who want to understand Chinese law, or translating English legal provisions into Chinese for the convenience of Chinese speakers who want to understand British or American law. These translations do not have any legal effect. (2) Translation itself with legal effect, such translated texts serving as legal texts and possessing legal effect. For example, signed contracts would become valid legal texts and would be legally binding on the parties concerned. The legal texts under study in this book refer to the second type of legal translation, i.e., regulatory legal texts such as laws and regulations, the Companies Ordinance of Hong Kong bilingual ordinances to be exact.

1.2 Legal translation

1.2.1 Overview of legal translation

With the acceleration of global economic integration, China plays a more active role in global affairs and interacts with countries around the world in such fields as politics, the economy, and culture more frequently. Therefore, diverse cross-border exchanges can only achieve positive development within the scope permitted by relevant national laws, which means that we must understand and comply with the different legal systems and legal institutions of various countries. In this context, the importance of legal translation becomes prominent and evident.

Wu (2002) believes that 'wherever there exist bilingual phenomena, legal issues may arise due to language problems ... Legal translation is a tool to ensure equality before the law for everyone.' According to Šarčević (1997: 1), 'Although translations of legal documents are among the oldest and most important in the world, legal translation has long been neglected in both translation and legal studies.' Despite having a longer history than bible translation, legal translation fails to draw sufficient attention. On the one hand, 'far from being recognised as an independent discipline, legal translation is regarded by translation theorists merely as one of the many subject areas of special-purpose translation, a branch of translation studies often snubbed for its alleged inferiority' (Šarčević, 1997: 1). Legal translation is of low status and inferior especially when compared with literary translation.

Nevertheless, legal translation has played a significant role throughout history in promoting interpersonal communication and exchanges between different cultures. Today, its importance is even more pronounced with the fast pace of globalisation. From a macro perspective, as the processes of globalisation and multilingualism accelerate, we live in an era of multiple languages coexisting and different social systems cohabitating. As a transnational and cross-regional means of communication, the role of translation is becoming increasingly significant.

For example, the functioning of the European Union heavily relies on translation. Similarly, Hong Kong, under its bilingual system, requires extensive translation of its legal ordinances since its sovereignty transfer and return to China in 1997. From a micro perspective, the increasing demand for the free flow of humans, goods, and capital means that legal translation, to some extent, affects each and every one of us. For instance, operating a business for a multinational company requires an understanding of the legal systems and regulations of other countries involved.

More importantly, legal translation differs from the translation of other types of texts as it carries legal effect. The misinterpretation or mistranslation of legal articles can lead to misunderstandings, disputes, or even wars. Therefore, legal translation plays a crucial role in safeguarding regional stability, world peace, and international order.

The importance of legal translation is fully demonstrated in the abundant research achievements in the field. Numerous scholars from both domestic and international contexts have made significant contributions to the study of legal translation, providing valuable guidance in terms of theory and practice (such as Šarčević, 1997; Alcaraz & Hughes, 2002; Cao, 2007; Li, 2007; Wang, 2006).

1.2.2 Features of legal translation

Legal terms are difficult and challenging, and some of them are not commonly seen in other text types. Legal sentences are long and complex, with many modifying clauses and phrases embedded. Those common features have come to the notice of many scholars. They have attempted to distinguish legal features from other text types, and have made efforts to summarise various features of legal texts.

Mellinkoff (1990: 11) summarises nine chief characteristics of the language of the law: (1) frequent use of common words with uncommon meanings; (2) frequent use of Old and Middle English words once in use but now rare; (3) frequent use of Latin words and phrases; (4) use of Old French and Anglo-Norman words which have not been taken into the general vocabulary; (5) use of terms of art; (6) use of argot; (7) frequent use of formal words; (8) deliberate use of words and expressions with flexible meanings; (9) attempts at extreme precision of expression.

Danet (1985) includes the following lexical features for legal texts: (1) common terms with uncommon meanings; (2) archaic expressions; (3) doublets; (4) formality; (5) unusual prepositional phrases; (6) frequency of 'any.' He also mentions syntactic features for legal texts: (1) nominalisations; (2) passives; (3) 'wh-' deletion; (4) conditionals; (5) prepositional phrases; (6) sentence length and complexity; (7) unique determiners; (8) impersonality; (9) negatives; (10) binomial expressions/parallel structures. Danet (1985) even points out prosodic features and discourse-level features of legal texts, which are rarely mentioned by other scholars.

These characteristics contribute to the distinctiveness of legal texts and reflect the specialised language and sentence structures used in the legal field.

1.2.3 Difficulties and challenges of legal translation

When speaking of legal translation, many people's first response is that it is overwhelmingly demanding and complicated. There are two main reasons: the first is the linguistic features of legal texts, and the second the different legal systems involved. Wang (2006: 8) suggests that the difficulty of legal translation depends primarily on the relationship between the two legal systems, with the relationship between the source language and the target language being of secondary importance. Cao (2007: 23) considers three factors that contribute to the difficulty of legal translation: systemic differences in law, linguistic differences, and cultural differences.

Generally speaking, legal translation involves three aspects:

(1) Language: since translation deals with two different languages, which may belong to different language families. For example, Chinese and English are significantly different in expression habits, sentence structures, and word usage. So, translators must be experts in both languages and proficient language users.
(2) Legal expertise: as legal translation belongs to the specific legal field, translators must have a solid understanding of legal knowledge, be aware of differences in legal systems, and have a grasp of the precise concepts and correct usage of legal terms in different legal systems in order to translate accurately and effectively.
(3) Translation: as a type of specialised translation, legal translation inevitably encounters issues that are also present in other translation domains, such as translation strategies or translation methods. Therefore, translators must be equipped with basic translation knowledge and translation skills.

In summary, legal translation involves language theory, legal expertise, and translation theory. Translators must address and resolve issues in those three aspects during the translation process, which makes legal translation more complex and challenging.

1.2.4 Legal translation in Hong Kong

Hong Kong's legal system belongs to the common law system, which originated from the accumulated precedents of the English courts since the Middle Ages. After the handover of Hong Kong to the People's Republic of China in 1997, the decision was made to implement the legal system of 'one country, two systems' in the Hong Kong Special Administrative Region (HKSAR). The successful operation of 'one country, two systems' relies not only on the cohesion of the national identity, history, and culture under the concept of 'one country' but also on mutual respect, communication, understanding, learning, cooperation, and complementarity between 'two systems.'

Not only is Hong Kong one of the few regions in the world that implements bilingual legislation, it is also the only jurisdiction in the world where legislation is enacted in both Chinese and English. Moreover, its history and cultural heritage are quite unique. In 1842, the signing of *The Treaty of Nanking* made Hong Kong a British colony. For over a hundred years, Hong Kong was under British rule and heavily influenced by British governance. Consequently, English naturally became the sole official language of Hong Kong. As law forms an integral part of a country or region's political system, Hong Kong's legal system gradually developed based on the British common law system. Significant changes in Hong Kong's legal history occurred in 1997 when Hong Kong returned to China on 1 July 1997. It was agreed that Hong Kong would maintain its common law system for at least 50 years after the handover. The establishment of a bilingual legal system had been under discussion for a decade prior to the handover, as mentioned by Yen Yuen Ho (cited in Luk, 2002: 3):

> In August 1986, *Hong Kong Royal Instructions* (i.e., the constitutional document under British rule) was revised to include the following provision: 'Laws may be enacted in either English or Chinese.' Seven months later, the Legislative Council of Hong Kong passed the Official Languages (Amendment) Ordinance, which supplemented the aforementioned revision. These revisions marked the beginning of implementing bilingual legislation in Hong Kong. The Official Languages (Amendment) Ordinance of 1987 stipulated that all new ordinances must be enacted in both Chinese and English as official languages. In April 1989, the first bilingual ordinance was introduced. Since then, all new ordinances (including subsidiary legislation) have been drafted and enacted in bilingual form, and all existing ordinances that were originally enacted only in English were 'translated' into Chinese by May 1997.

According to Section 4(1) of the Official Languages (Amendment) Ordinance of 1987, 'All ordinances shall be enacted and promulgated in both official languages.' At that time, Hong Kong had over 500 main ordinances and approximately 1,000 subsidiary ordinances. Before May 1997, the Law Drafting Division of the Department of Justice and the Bilingual Legislation Consultative Committee translated all the ordinances into Chinese. According to the newly added Section 10B(1), both the Chinese and English versions of the ordinances are deemed 'equally authentic.' In May 1998, the Law Drafting Division of the Department of Justice stated in the revised 'Discussion Paper on Dealing with Discrepancies in the Two Languages of Ordinances' that, 'Whether the Chinese version of an ordinance is promulgated simultaneously with the English version or subsequently declared as authentic, the Chinese version must be interpreted as having equal effect and authority as the English version' (cited in Luk, 2002: 354). Despite the provision in Section 10B(1) and the statement from the Department of Justice, Cheung Tat Ming (cited in Luk, 2002: 354–356) argues that:

> The Chinese version is a translation derived from the original English ordinances, and it is not a newly enacted legislative text. The English version is

> the original version of the ordinance and has long existed … From the legal perspective, if the Chinese version is declared authentic after the English version is enacted, in case of discrepancies in the textual meaning between the English and Chinese versions, the English version should prevail … If it is indeed intended to grant equal status and authenticity to both language versions, the only legally sound approach would be to repeal all ordinances originally enacted in a single language and re-enact them in bilingual form. Attempting to achieve bilingual legislation through translation of ordinances is unlikely to be entirely successful.

We should note that this perspective represents Cheung's opinion on the matter and may not necessarily reflect the views of all legal experts or the current interpretation and implementation of bilingual legislation in Hong Kong.

Therefore, in order to address the potential discrepancies between the English and Chinese authentic texts, the Hong Kong legislation has established the following two interpretative provisions (cited in Luk, 2002: 4):

> Where a term or clause in the English text of an ordinance corresponds to a term or clause in the Chinese text, the term or clause in the ordinance shall be construed in accordance with its meaning in the common law. Where, upon the comparison of the two authentic texts of an ordinance, a discrepancy in meaning arises and the application of the usual rules of statutory interpretation does not resolve the discrepancy, the meaning of the ordinance shall be determined by having regard to the purpose and effect of the ordinance and adopting the interpretation that best reconciles and harmonises the meanings of the two texts.

Translating Hong Kong's English legal ordinances into Chinese is indeed a challenging task. This is due to the fact that English legal terminology is rooted in the English legal system and reflects the social and cultural background of that system's evolution, making it difficult to accurately translate into Chinese. Additionally, there are semantic, grammatical, and syntactic differences between the Chinese and English languages, making it challenging for the Chinese translation to fully achieve the legal effect of the English legal ordinances. Furthermore, Hong Kong's legal ordinances are based on outdated British regulations, many of which were written in archaic and complex English, further complicating the task of translation into Chinese.

In fact, the translation of Hong Kong's legal texts has drawn the attention of several scholars. For instance, Jordan (1997) raised the question of how to reconcile Hong Kong's existing capitalist common law legal system with China's current socialist civil law legal system after the handover in 1997. Translating Hong Kong's ordinances into Chinese poses various challenges. Firstly, the conceptual, structural, and ideological differences between China's socialist legal system and relevant aspects of British common law make translation particularly difficult. Secondly, translators need to address the differences between the Chinese and

English languages. Šarčević (1997: 273) expressed her views on the difficulties of translating Hong Kong's legal texts, pointing out the historical, conceptual, and ideological differences between Hong Kong's capitalist common law and China's socialist system, as well as the linguistic and cultural differences between Chinese and English. Additionally, there are differences in spoken and written expressions between Hong Kong and mainland China. All of these factors make it challenging for translators to achieve consistency and equivalence in terms of meaning, effect, and intention.

1.2.5 Plain language movement and its influence on legal translation

The plain language movement is a recent language movement that has been launched in countries like the United States and the United Kingdom, aiming to address the issue of obscure and difficult-to-understand English documents. In the 1970s, there were concerns in the United States regarding the lengthy, convoluted, repetitive, and complex language used in the terms and conditions of cashier's cheques, which made it impossible for customers to understand their rights and obligations. Even some lawyers and judges found it challenging to comprehend. In response, a ground-breaking law called the Plain Language Law was passed in the state of New York in 1977 and implemented in 1978. The then-president James Earl Carter Jr. urged federal government departments to ensure that every regulation they issued was written in clear and understandable English, so that those who had to comply with the laws could comprehend them. In other words, the United States advocated for the use of language that is easy to understand and discouraged unnecessary verbosity. Subsequently, with the increased awareness of government services and the introduction of the concept of public access to information, the plain language movement further expanded to encompass other fields, including law, finance, business, healthcare, etc. The movement seeks to promote the use of plain and comprehensible language to enhance communication between organisations and individuals.

The plain language movement has gained particular urgency in the legal field, where a multitude of specialised terminology and convoluted sentence structures in legal texts often leave laymen perplexed. 'Legalese is typically criticised for being overly complicated, dense, repetitive, and outdated … "Plain English" has established itself as a reform movement focused on making legal language more accessible, in particular to non-lawyers' (Candlin et al., 2002: 303). 'These words are not genuine terms of art because they have no special or precise legal meaning. They are now considered stilted and archaic by almost every authority on legal writing and are derisively labelled "legalese"' (Dworsky, 1990: 3). Clearly, promoting the plain language movement not only facilitates understanding of legal language but also benefits the work of legal translators, as translated texts would be less obscure and difficult to comprehend than the original.

However, it is evident that the implementation of the plain language movement in Hong Kong lags behind that of European and American countries. Many lawyers and legal document drafters in Hong Kong continue to use archaic terms and convoluted sentence structures. There are two main reasons: first, legal professionals themselves may not genuinely support the plain language movement because if clients can understand legal provisions on their own, there would be less need for lawyers' services, resulting in a significant reduction in their income. Second, the Hong Kong government has not shown the same level of commitment as the US government in promoting the plain language movement. This situation has, to a certain extent, contributed to the obscurity and lack of simplicity in legal English writing and translation in Hong Kong. One of the objectives of this book is to analyse Hong Kong's bilingual legislation and derive translation patterns to alleviate the workload of translators when they translate conditional clauses in legal texts. It is also intended to encourage legal document drafters to use clear and understandable legal language, thereby promoting the plain language movement in Hong Kong to some extent.

1.3 Data source and research object

The corpus used in this study is derived from the Companies Ordinance of the Hong Kong bilingual ordinances (online Hong Kong e-Legislation). The Hong Kong bilingual ordinances comprise over 1,000 ordinances or chapters, and these ordinances and subsidiary legislation are provided by the Department of Justice of the Hong Kong government. They can be accessed from the website of the Bilingual Laws Information System. The Companies Ordinance consists of 15 subchapters. However, this study focuses only on the main body of the legislation, specifically the content of Sections 1 to 367. The bilingual versions of the main body of this Companies Ordinance contain over 600,000 words. The foundation of this legal system is the Companies Ordinance enacted in 1933, which is Chapter 32 of the Laws of Hong Kong. This ordinance has undergone multiple amendments over time and Chapter 32 was renewed as Chapter 622 in 2014 (the usage and translation of introductory words for conditional clauses are found to be similar). The version of the Companies Ordinance analysed in this book is based on the content updated on the website of the Department of Justice of Hong Kong as of January 2010 (as the Hong Kong laws are continually updated based on the promulgation or repeal of regulations). It is worth noting that the text data used in this book is sourced from electronic materials available on the website of the Department of Justice of Hong Kong, which differs from traditional printed texts and therefore is more convenient for data collection and analysis.

In modern society, companies are not only tools for conducting business activities but also fundamental entities in economic relations and central to society. The reasonableness of a company's structure, its adherence to proper conduct, and the effectiveness of its operations directly impact the balance of socio-economic order and economic efficiency in society. Therefore, it is crucial to regulate companies through legal adjustments. Whether in countries or regions with a civil law or common law tradition, the majority of them regulate companies through enacted company laws. This is especially true in Hong Kong, a place known for its limited land and high property values, where a significant number of companies are established and listed each year. Therefore, there is a greater need for comprehensive regulations to legally govern all aspects of a company's activities. As an international business and financial centre, Hong Kong has a well-established system of company laws. It not only meets the demands and needs of the local business community but also caters to the requirements and needs of specialised companies established for investment and project financing activities in this Asia's second-largest stock market.

Hong Kong's company law consists of two parts: statutory law (in English) and case law (in English). Initially, the statutory law closely followed that of the UK, and the case law was also derived from the UK and other Commonwealth jurisdictions. However, Hong Kong has now developed its own local statutory and case law, with the Companies Ordinance being the longest and most extensive legislation in Hong Kong. The Companies Ordinance has wide-ranging applicability, not only to local companies but also to overseas companies. It applies not only to private companies but also to publicly listed companies. Furthermore, it applies to individual companies, group companies, and holding companies, as well as subsidiary companies.

The focus of this study is the conditional clauses in the Companies Ordinance of the Hong Kong bilingual ordinances. The reasons for choosing it as the research subject are listed below:

(1) Hong Kong is a business-oriented society with numerous new companies being established every year, and there is a significant number of litigation cases related to corporate affairs. Therefore, the Companies Ordinance holds great importance in Hong Kong.
(2) Through research on several law firm websites in Hong Kong, it is found that the Companies Ordinance is one of the most frequently used and cited ordinances in Hong Kong.
(3) The Companies Ordinance serves as a substantial corpus for analysis, consisting of 367 sections, making it the longest legislation among the 1,117 ordinances in Hong Kong.
(4) As it is unnecessary to analyse every single sentence in the entire Companies Ordinance, this study focuses specifically on conditional clauses, which account for approximately 44% of all the sentences in the legislation. This is because the purpose of law drafting is to set a certain action pattern, which makes it common to have a large amount of 'if' conditional clauses—a certain action or condition results in a certain result. Conditional clauses play a significant role in legal texts, and understanding the translation patterns of these clauses can greatly enhance the efficiency of understanding and translating legal texts.
(5) The Companies Ordinance has not yet been extensively studied as a corpus (in contrast to the Basic Law which is frequently used), thus the research findings and conclusions derived from this study will not duplicate existing research.

Considering these five reasons, it is believed that researching the translation of conditional clauses in the Companies Ordinance is meaningful. The aim of this study is to provide translators with various translations and patterns for conditional clauses through an analysis of the conditional clauses in the ordinance.

1.4 Research methodology

1.4.1 Descriptive research approach

The descriptive research method is employed in this study. As we know, traditional translation studies are mostly prescriptive. Prescriptive research involves value judgements based on subjective ideas, dealing with 'good or bad' or 'should and should not.' Descriptive research presents collected data and information in an objective manner, describing who, what, when, where, and how. In contrast to prescription, description is objective, rational, and empirical, without value judgements (Chu, 2009: 5).

Descriptive research was originally proposed by the Israeli scholar Toury. He abandoned the traditional prescriptive framework and viewed translation from a different perspective. He believed that the essence of translation studies should be empirical and that translation should start with describing translation phenomena. Toury (1995) proposed in his book that descriptive studies should be conducted on translation practices and translation outcomes, rather than imposing prescriptions or judgements on translation. Therefore, the traditional prescriptive approach in translation studies has flaws since it often imposes various prescriptions or standards on translation, implying subjective judgements of what constitutes good or bad translation and prescribing what translators should or should not do. But in practice, translators often find such prescriptions or standards impractical or unattainable.

Holmes (1972) put forward his ideas on 'The Name and Nature of Translation Studies,' that is, translation studies should be regarded as an independent discipline. He also emphasised that, as an empirical discipline, translation research focuses more on empirical facts and less on abstract theoretical generalisations. In Toury's words,

> empirical disciplines are devised to account, in a systematic and controlled way, for particular segments of the 'real world'. Consequently, no empirical science can make a claim for completeness and (relative) autonomy unless it has a proper descriptive branch. Describing, explaining and predicting phenomena pertaining to its object level is thus the main goal of such a discipline.
> (1995: 1)

Toury held that 'what constitutes the subject matter of a proper discipline of Translation Studies is (observable or reconstructable) facts of real life rather than merely speculative entities resulting from preconceived hypotheses and theoretical models' (1995: 1). Descriptive research also evidences that translation studies is empirical because it avoids subjective inferences and prescriptive statements, making theoretical research in translation studies more objective and scientific. The descriptive branch is the most fundamental and important branch in translation studies because its research findings provide specific data and evidence for theoretical and applied research. Descriptive translation studies contribute to translation studies by accumulating descriptions of translation phenomena in different cultures and periods, helping researchers approach the essence of translation and understand the translation concepts.

1.4.2 Method of mixing quantitative and qualitative analysis

To be specific, this study adopts a combination of qualitative and quantitative analysis. The mixed mode of quantitative and qualitative analysis was proposed by Bryman (1988). The purpose of combining these two approaches is to draw on the strengths of both and make up for their respective shortcomings. Quantitative research is the process of collecting and analysing numerical data, which can be used to find patterns and averages, make predictions, test causal relationships, and generalise results to wider populations. More specifically, it refers to the collection of data or information primarily in numerical form, followed by the quantification, testing, and analysis of the data to obtain meaningful conclusions. Based on certain standards, it aims to measure and compare the numerical values of the research subject or to determine the patterns of certain factors. Qualitative research, the opposite of qualitative research, involves collecting and analysing non-numerical data. Widely adopted by researchers to define and address research questions, it focuses on exploring issues, understanding event phenomena, analysing human behaviours and perspectives, and providing insightful answers. To sum up, quantitative research answers the question of 'what,' while qualitative research addresses the question of 'why.' By combining both qualitative and quantitative approaches, this study aims to gain a comprehensive insight into the research topic by utilising the strengths of each method.

Translation studies in general rely heavily on qualitative research, and this study is no exception as it involves analysing conditional clauses in Hong Kong legal texts. However, if certain patterns or tendencies are to be identified, substantial data is needed to substantiate the findings. In other words, if specific translation patterns for conditional clauses are to be proved, the quantitative research method is essential to support the identified patterns. Therefore, this study adopts the mixed mode of qualitative and quantitative research to provide a better understanding of the translation of conditional clauses in legal translation.

1.4.3 Data analytical method and research steps

In this study, a simple random sampling method is employed for the specific text analysis of conditional clauses. There are two reasons. Firstly, legal texts exhibit certain similarities in content and form (compared with literary works), and using random sampling helps to avoid analysing highly similar sentences, thus saving time and effort. Secondly, the research focuses on conditional clauses in the Companies

Ordinance, which constitute a significant proportion. For instance, there are over 1,500 instances of conditional clauses introduced by 'if' and 'where.' Therefore, the use of a random sampling method facilitates the analysis and ensures practicality. A brief introduction to the sampling research method is introduced below.

In statistics, sampling is an inferential statistical method that involves selecting a subset of individuals, known as a sample, from a target population (also referred to as the population or the parent population). By observing certain attributes of the sample, reliable estimations and judgements about the quantitative characteristics of the population can be made, thus gaining insights into the population. Prior to sampling, the population is divided into sampling units, which are non-overlapping and collectively represent the population. Each individual in the population belongs to only one unit.

There are various sampling methods available, including simple random sampling, systematic sampling, stratified sampling, and cluster sampling. In this study, simple random sampling is employed. Simple random sampling, also known as pure random sampling, involves selecting n units from a population consisting of N units in such a way that each of the C^n_N possible samples has an equal chance to be selected. Therefore, the probability of each unit being selected is $1/C^n_N$ (Hu & Sun, 2000: 5). The feature of this sampling method is that each sampling unit has an equal chance of being selected, and the units in the sample are completely independent of each other, without any predetermined associations or exclusions.

As far as this study is concerned, the research object of this study, the Companies Ordinance, is divided into several sampling units. The Companies Ordinance consists of 367 sections, each addressing different aspects of the ordinance. To ensure coverage of the entire Company Ordinance, the author adopts a systematic sampling approach, selecting conditional clauses introduced by 'if,' 'where,' and 'in (the) case' that appear in every fifth section (e.g., sections 5, 10, 15, and so on) for analysis. This sampling approach allows for the representation of conditional clauses found throughout the entire Companies Ordinance while maintaining feasibility.

In this study, the research steps for analysing conditional clauses are as follows:

(1) Identify various types of conditional clauses present in the English source text and calculate the frequency of usage for each introductory word for conditional clauses.
(2) Analyse translations used for the main introductory words for conditional clauses, including 'if,' 'where,' 'when,' 'in (the) case,' and 'in the event,' so as to examine whether different translations achieve the same function as the original text and compare the similarities and differences among these introductory words.
(3) Given that 'if' and 'where' are the most used introductory words for conditional clauses in the Companies Ordinance, this study focuses on these two groups of conditional clauses by using a sampling method, in order to explore the translation patterns or regularities of conditional clauses.

1.4.4 Research questions

This book focuses on the following four research questions:

(1) What are the introductory words for conditional clauses and their corresponding translations found in the Companies Ordinance?
(2) What are the differences in usage and translation between the introductory words for conditional clauses: 'if,' 'where,' 'when,' 'in (the) case,' and 'in the event'?
(3) Do the different Chinese translations of the introductory words for conditional clauses achieve the same function as the original text?
(4) Does the translation of conditional clauses in the Companies Ordinance follow specific patterns?

By addressing these questions, the study aims to provide a comprehensive understanding of the translation of conditional clauses in the context of the Companies Ordinance and explore potential patterns in their translation.

1.5 Research significance

This study is meaningful in the following three aspects.

Firstly, based on the theoretical framework of translation typology, this book summarises traditional translation typology and puts forward a new perspective on legal text translation typology. From this new perspective, the types of legal texts should be determined based on whether the functions of the source text and the target text are consistent. When the function of the target text is the same as that of the source text, the legal text is vocative. But when the function of the target text differs from that of the source text, the source text is vocative, while the target text can be either informative or expressive. This can be seen as a supplementary contribution to the theory of text typology for translation.

Secondly, during the analysis of conditional clauses in legal texts, a simple random sampling method is employed to analyse a portion of the conditional clauses in the Companies Ordinance. Based on the analysis, translation patterns are identified for dominant conditional clauses introduced by 'if' and 'where.' Through a comparison of translations of different introductory words for conditional clauses, the similarities and differences among these introductory words are examined.

Last but not least, based on the fact that the bilingual legal text in Hong Kong belongs to the vocative type, the most crucial aspect is the function, i.e., the translation must achieve the same function or intention as the original text. In this study, conclusive generalisations are made by examining the translations of different introductory words for conditional clauses in the Companies Ordinance, so as to determine whether various translations of the introductory words for conditional clauses achieve the same function as the original text.

1.6 Overall framework of the book

This book consists of six chapters in total:

- Chapter 1 introduces the research background, gives an overview of the status quo of legal translation, highlights the significance of this study, and presents the data source and research methodology used in this book.
- Chapter 2 presents a literature review, discussing the current research of legal translation and specifically focusing on the study of conditional clauses in legal texts. It emphasises the necessity of enhancing the research on the translation of conditional clauses in legal texts.
- Chapter 3 adopts translation typology as the theoretical framework, summarising the traditional viewpoints of translation typology and applying them to the analysis of legal texts. Based on this foundation, a new view is proposed on the types of legal texts, which serves as a theoretical reference for the analysis of conditional clause translation in Chapter 4.
- Chapter 4 conducts a descriptive analysis of conditional clauses in the Companies Ordinance, with the aim of identifying different translations of various introductory words for conditional clauses and investigating whether these translations achieve the same function as the original text.
- Chapter 5, based on the analysis in Chapter 4, summarises different translation patterns for conditional clauses introduced by 'if' and 'where.' Then the usage and translation of the conditional clauses introduced by 'if' and 'where' are exemplified by different analytical methods.
- Chapter 6, the concluding chapter, summarises the findings of this research, explains the significance of these results, points out the limitations of the study, and explores directions for future research.

References

Alcaraz Varó, Enrique & Hughes, Brain. *Legal Translation Explained.* Manchester; Northampton: St. Jerome Publishing, 2002.

Bryman, Alan. *Quantity and Quality in Social Research.* London: Routledge, 1988.

Cao, Deborah. *Translating Law.* Clevedon; Buffalo: Multilingual Matters, 2007.

Candlin, C.N., Bhatia, V.K., & Jensen, C.H. Developing legal writing materials for English second language learners: Problems and perspectives. *English for Specific Purposes,* 2002(21): 299–320.

Danet, Brenda. Legal discourse. In Teun A. Van Dijk (ed.), *Handbook of Discourse Analysis* Vol 1. Orlando: Academic Press, Inc., Harcourt Brace Jovanovich Publishers, 1985.

Dworsky, Alan L. *The Little Book on Legal Writing.* Littleton: F.B. Rothman, 1990.

Gibbons, John. *Forensic Linguistics: An Introduction to Language in the Justice System.* Malden, MA: Blackwell Publishing, 2003.

Goodrich, Peter. *Legal Discourse: Studies in Linguistics, Rhetoric, and Legal Analysis.* Basingstoke: Macmillan, 1987.

Holmes, James. 1972. The name and nature of translation studies. In Venuti Lawrence (ed.). *The Translation Studies Reader.* London; New York: Routledge, 2000: 172–185.

Jordan, Ann D. Lost in the Translation: Two legal cultures, the common law judiciary and the basic law of the Hong Kong special administrative region. *Cornell International Law Journal*, 1997(2): 335–380.

Mellinkoff, David. *The Language of the Law*. Boston: Little, Brown and Company, 1990.

Šarčević, Susan. *New Approach to Legal Translation*. The Hague; Boston: Kluwer Law International, 1997.

Toury, Gideon. *Descriptive Translation Studies and Beyond*. Amsterdam; Philadelphia: John Benjamins Publishing Company, 1995.

Chu, Chiyu [朱志瑜]. 翻譯研究:規定、描寫、倫理 [Translation studies: Prescription, description, and ethics]. 中國翻譯[*Chinese Translators Journal*], 2009(3): 5–12, 95.

He, Jiuying, Wang, Ning, & Dong, Kun [何九盈、王寧、董琨]. 辭源 [*Ciyuan*]. 香港：商務出版社 [The Commercial Press (Hong Kong) Ltd.], 1979–1984.

Hu, Jianying & Sun, Shanze [胡健穎、孫山澤]. 抽樣調查的理論、方法和應用 [*Theories, Approaches and Application of Sampling Survey*]. 北京：北京大學出版社 [Beijing: Peking University Press], 2000.

Li, Kexing [李克興]. 法律翻譯理論與實踐 [*Legal Translation: A Theoretical and Practical Approach*]. 北京：北京大學出版社 [Beijing: Peking University Press], 2007.

Li, Kexing & Zhang, Xinhong [李克興、張新紅]. 法律文本與法律翻譯 [*Legal Texts and Legal Translation*]. 北京：中國對外翻譯出版公司 [Beijing: China Translation & Publishing Corporation], 2005.

Luk, Man Wai [陆文慧]. 法律翻譯：從實踐出發 [*Legal Translation in Practice*]. 香港：中華書局 [Hong Kong: Chung Hwa Book Co.], 2002.

Wang, Daogeng [王道庚]. 法律翻譯：理論與實踐 [*Legal Translation – Theory and Practice*]. 香港：香港城市大學出版社 [Hong Kong: City University of Hong Kong Press], 2006.

Wu, Weiping [吳偉平].語言與法律—司法領域的語言學研究 [*Language and the Law: Linguistic Research in the Legal Field*]. 上海：上海外語教育出版社 [Shanghai: Shanghai Foreign Language Education Press], 2002.

Online Hong Kong e-Legislation: https://www.elegislation.gov.hk

2 Literature review

2.1 Reviewing studies on legal translation

This section reviews relevant studies on legal translation, categorising existing research achievements in legal translation into four aspects: translation of legal terms, features of legal language, theories, principles, and methods of legal translation, and text types of legal texts.

2.1.1 Reviewing translation of legal terms

Legal language and legal translation cover a substantial number of specialised terms and vocabulary. Legal terminology refers to the legal concepts defined by legal provisions, and its prominent feature is that its meaning is conferred by the law, which means it is fixed and unique. Scholars have proposed principles and strategies for translating legal terms.

For instance, Zhu (2002) suggests four basic principles for translating legal specialised terms: firstly, correctly understanding the precise meaning of the term in its original context; secondly, seeking equivalent or closely equivalent specialised terms in the domestic legal system as much as possible; thirdly, translating non-equivalent terms as neutral terms used in non-specialised legal language, to avoid confusion and ambiguity; and finally, translating ambiguous terms as ambiguous terms, to keep ambiguity in the original. Li (2005) explores specific translation methods for legal terms based on four lexical characteristics: speciality, formality, objectivity, and accuracy.

Some scholars have explored the translation of specific legal words. For example, Li (2007) provides a comprehensive analysis and summary of the modal verbs 'shall,' 'must,' and 'may' in legal texts, including their negative forms, which express prohibitions in legal texts. Lin and Ji (2002) analyse the '的' (de; of) structure in legal texts and classify it into eight categories: 'whoever' structure, 'anyone who' structure, 'no one who' structure, subject-identifying structure, subject-completing structure, 'where + person' structure, 'where + things' structure, and 'if it is + adjective' structure. Xin (2003) suggests that the translation of the names of laws and regulations should be carefully examined and studied, i.e., attempting to achieve fidelity when translating Chinese laws and regulations, and faithfully reproducing the original text equivalent to the foreign treaties, agreements, or

DOI: 10.4324/9781003359180-2

laws when translating them. Qu and Xing (2005) analyse the translation of terms such as 'article, paragraph, subparagraph, and item' in legal translation. Besides, *Translating Legal Language* (Chen, 1998) and *Translation Talks in the Legal Garden* (Chen, 2000) provide vivid and interesting examples of various translation phenomena observed.

It can be observed that the above-mentioned studies mainly focus on the translation of legal terminology, while there is relatively less discussion on the sentence and textual levels. As Šarčević (1997) noted, most scholars noticed the importance of legal terms because specialised legal terminology can better reflect the typical characteristics of a legal system or constitution (Du, Zhang & Yuan, 2004). Therefore, much of the research has been on the terminology aspect, with relatively less research on textual and pragmatic aspects. In other words, compared with micro-level research, macro-level research in this area is relatively scarce (Šarčević, 1997: 2). This book primarily focuses on the translation of conditional clauses in legal texts, addressing the gap in research at the macro level.

2.1.2 Reviewing features of legal language

In addition to the abundant research papers on legal terminology, scholars have focused extensively on the linguistic features of legal texts. According to Cao (2007: 23), 'Legal language is not a universal technical language but one that is tied to a national system, very different from the language used in pure science, say mathematics or physics.' Legal language exhibits significant differences compared with other types of language.

The following are the primary characteristics of legal language in terms of vocabulary and syntactic structure put forward by some Western scholars.

Cao (2007: 53) emphasises the following four aspects of lexical features in legal translation: (1) legal conceptual issues and the question of the equivalence and non-equivalence of legal concepts in translation; (2) legal terms that are bound to law and legal institutions; (3) legal language as a technical language in terms of ordinary vs. legal meanings, and legal synonyms; and (4) terminological difficulties arising from linguistic uncertainty such as vagueness and ambiguity. Alcaraz and Hughes (2002: 5) highlight the main lexical features of legal English, including Latinisms, terms of French or Noman origin, formal register and archaic diction, archaic adverbs and prepositional phrases, redundancy (doublets and triplets), frequency of performative verbs, and changing registers (euphemisms and contemporary colloquialism) . They (2002: 18) also suggest six syntactic features of legal English, including unusually long sentences, anfractuosity of English legal syntax, abundant use of the passive voice, conditionals and hypothetical formulations, simple syntax of plain judicial narrative, and active and passive parties in legal relationships (the suffixes -er/-or and -ee). Mellinkoff (1990) also summarises nine lexical features, including common words with specialised legal meanings, rare words from Old and Middle English, Latin words and phrases, specialised French words, terms of art, professional jargon, formal expressions, words with flexible meanings, and attempts at extreme precision. Bhatia (1993: 106–113) presents the syntactic features of legal provisions, including sentence length, nominal character, complex prepositional phrases, binominal and multinomial expressions, initial case descriptions, qualifications in legislative provisions, and syntactic discontinuities. Gibbons (2003: 166) discusses a wide range of issues on language and law, with a focus on the technical and specialised nature of legal language. These scholars provide valuable insights into the unique features of legal language, both in terms of vocabulary and sentence structures.

Furthermore, a number of Chinese scholars have provided detailed descriptions of the characteristics of legal language.

Chen (2007: 10–15) identifies several prominent lexical features in legal English, including specialised terminology, conversion of common words into specialised words, formal vocabulary, Old English, loanwords, nominalisation of verbs, ambiguous terms, and the use of synonyms. Additionally, he summarises the syntactic features of legal language, such as long sentences with complex sentence structures, passive voice, declarative sentences (predominant in legal English, with fewer imperative, interrogative, and exclamatory sentences), complete sentences (with comprehensive, detailed, and precise information), 'if' sentences, 'shall' sentences, parallel sentence structures (commonly used in provisions to regulate), and common patterns (e.g., patterns using 'means,' 'includes,' and 'refers to') (2007: 16–24). Ji (1999) opines that legal English is the most formal style among various English genres, characterised by the use of specialised terminology, archaic words, loanwords, parallel words, and the use of 'shall.' Xiao (2001) mentions that the origins of English-Chinese legal terms include keeping old legal terms, creating new legal terms, adopting loanwords, and transforming general vocabulary into legal terms within a common language. Wang (2003) acknowledges that apart from the impact of lexical features on legal translation in English, differences in cultural background can also pose challenges to legal translation. The divergences in writing, word usage, and syntax between English and Chinese due to cultural differences can create enormous difficulties. Furthermore, the translator's legal and cultural knowledge has an impact on legal translation, and the translator is required to have a sufficient understanding of different legal systems and related aspects. The insights provided by these Chinese scholars contribute to a comprehensive understanding of the characteristics of legal language and the challenges they pose for translation.

To sum up, the descriptions of the characteristics of legal language mentioned above provide valuable guidance for translators in the process of translating legal texts. They also highlight the requirements placed on legal translators, emphasising the need to pay attention to the specific features of legal language. Although the inherent features of legal English make legal translation particularly challenging, translators who are familiar with the lexical characteristics and syntactic patterns of legal language will undoubtedly be more efficient and effective in their translation process.

2.1.3 Reviewing theories, principles, and methods of legal translation

Various scholars have put forward their views on the translation principles for legal texts. For example, Du (2004) mentions three fundamental principles to consider in legal translation: fairness, accuracy, and appropriateness. Qiu (2000) asserts that legal texts emphasise accuracy and precision, and have strict requirements for vocabulary, syntactic structures, and register. Therefore, the translation of legal texts should adhere to the following principles: the use of solemn words, accuracy, conciseness, consistency in terminology, and the use of specialised terminology. Li (1997: 176), based on the analysis of major issues in legal translation and the characteristics of legal writing, summarises six practical principles for legal translation: accuracy and precision, consistency and identity, clarity and conciseness, professionalism, standardised language, and teamwork. These principles proposed by scholars provide important guidance for translators in translating legal texts, ensuring that the translation is faithful, accurate, and appropriate to the legal context.

In addition to the general principles of legal translation, many scholars have proposed specific translation methods. Chen (2007: 34), based on the characteristics of legal language and its specific legal functions, suggests that legal translation should follow the principles of accuracy, precision, standardisation, and consistency. Fu (2002) emphasises the need for precision in translating legal contracts, suggesting that when translating from Chinese to English, the choice of words should be formal, precise, and distinct. These specific translation methods proposed by scholars take into account the unique features and functions of legal language, providing translators with practical guidelines to ensure accurate and equivalent translations of legal texts.

These translation principles and methods undoubtedly provide guidance for translating legal texts. However, their limitation lies in the fact that they are prescriptive rather than objectively derived from the description. Therefore, this book adopts a descriptive research method to analyse the conditional clauses in the Companies Ordinance in Hong Kong. This method yields more scientific and objective conclusions, and the translation patterns derived are highly applicable to practical translation. In this regard, compared with the aforementioned traditional prescriptive principles and methods, conclusions based on descriptive research are more practical for legal translation.

2.1.4 Reviewing text typology of legal texts

Apart from the above research focusing on specific aspects, scholars like Li and Zhang (2005) have systematically described the issues of legal translation from the perspective of text typology. While foreign translation theorists such as Nord and Newmark mentioned the text typology of legal texts, they did not delve into specific issues of legal translation. Chen (2007) explores the translation of legal genres from the angles of stylistics, pragmatics, and rhetoric, which expands the research field of legal translation to some extent and has practical significance in guiding the improvement of translation efficiency and quality in specific legal translation practices. Besides, there are research works that do not involve legal translation theory but aim to impart practical skills, such as Sun (2003, 2004) and Wang (2006). It is worth mentioning that among numerous works on legal translation, Šarčević's book *New Approach to Legal Translation* (1997) provides the most systematic and comprehensive discussion on legal translation. The first half of the book introduces the special status of legal translation, the history of legal translation, and the role of legal translators, while the second half primarily focuses on the legal knowledge that translators need to possess in legal translation and how to handle the issues encountered in legal translation. These various research works contribute to the understanding and development of legal translation theory and practice, offering valuable insights and guidelines for researchers and practitioners in the field.

2.2 Reviewing studies on conditional clauses

This section first introduces various classifications of conditional clauses. It then focuses on discussing the current research status of conditional clauses and their translation in legal texts, based on which the research significance of this study will be highlighted.

2.2.1 Introduction of conditional clauses

In contrast to main clauses, subordinate clauses are subordinate to a main clause and cannot function as independent sentences. In English, there are three main types of subordinate clauses: noun clauses (including subject clauses, object clauses, predicative clauses, and appositive clauses), adjective clauses (also known as relative clauses), and adverbial clauses (including clauses of time, condition, result, purpose, reason, concession, place, manner, etc.). Adverbial clauses primarily modify the main clause or the predicate of the main clause. According to *A Comprehensive Grammar of the English Language* (Quirk et al., 1985), adverbial clauses can be categorised as clauses of place, time, condition, reason, result, degree, concession, manner, comparison, purpose, and exception. When we speak of conditional clauses, most people immediately think of sentences introduced by 'if' or the Chinese sentence pattern '如果 …… 那麼 ……' (rú guǒ …… nà me ……; if … then …). But are there other introductory words besides 'if'? Are there other sentence types of conditional clauses? In natural language, the conditional subordinate clause is mainly used to establish a certain situation, while the following clause describes what would happen based on that situation. Although we often express conditional relationships by using the compound sentence pattern 'if … then,' this sentence pattern, strictly speaking, is not always a conditional clause. This is because in some sentence patterns, there is no direct cause-and-effect relationship between the premise and the conclusion. A detailed explanation of types of conditional clauses will be introduced below.

A systematic description of English conditional clauses can be found in various sources, including earlier works such as *The English Verb* (Palmer, 1974: 142–151) and *A Comprehensive Grammar of the English Language* (Quirk et al., 1985: 1088–1097), as well as more recent works such as *The Cambridge Grammar of the English Language* (Huddleston & Pullum, 2002) and *Cambridge Grammar of English: A Comprehensive Guide: Spoken and Written English Grammar and*

Usage (Carter & McCarthy, 2006). With regard to the classification of 'if' conditional clauses, there are three main classifications in grammar:

(1) Conditional clauses are divided into two categories: real conditionals and unreal conditionals. Real conditionals are further subdivided into factual conditionals and non-factual conditionals (non-factual conditionals are also known as counterfactual conditionals).
(2) Conditional clauses are divided into two categories: direct conditionals and indirect conditionals.
(3) Conditional clauses are divided into open conditional construction and remote conditional construction.

In connection with the first classification, the Chinese scholar Zhang (1989: 1161–1165) adopts Palmer's viewpoint and proposes that conditional clauses, based on whether the content or situation is factual or likely to be realised, can be classified into real conditionals and unreal conditionals, which falls into the first classification. In a typical real conditional clause, the content of the subordinate clause serves as the reason and basis for the realisation of the situation in the main clause, and the content of the main and subordinate clauses cannot be regarded as two logically unrelated propositions. But in terms of an unreal conditional clause, the relationship between the main and subordinate clauses is not as close as that in real conditional clauses (Xu, 2005).

With respect to the second classification, Quirk et al. (1985: 1088) divide conditional clauses into direct conditionals and indirect conditionals, stating that,

> The central uses of conditional clauses express a direct condition: they convey that the situation in the matrix clause is directly contingent on that of the conditional clause. Put another way, the truth of the proposition in the matrix clause is a consequence of the fulfilment of the condition in the conditional clause … More peripheral use of conditional clauses expresses an indirect condition. The condition is not related to the situation in the matrix clause.

Two examples provided can better illustrate these two situations:

Example 1: If you put the baby down, she'll scream.
Chinese translation: 如果你把嬰兒放下，她就會尖叫。
In this sentence, the truth of the main clause 'she'll scream' is contingent on the realisation of the condition 'your putting the baby down', or it can be understood as 'If you don't put the baby down, she won't scream.'

Example 2: She's far too considerate, if I may say so.
Chinese translation: 她太體貼了，如果我可以這麼說。
In this sentence, the truth of the assertion in the main clause 'She's far too considerate' is not dependent on agreement from the listener.

In respect of the third classification, Huddleston and Pullum (2002: 738) propose that a typical conditional construction consists of a protasis (conditional clause) and an apodosis (consequent clause). The distinction between open and remote conditional constructions lies in the fact that the latter often describes situations that differ from reality. For example, 'If you are under 18, you need parental approval.' This is an open conditional construction. However, 'If you were under 18, you would need parental approval' is a remote conditional construction (2002: 748). The first and second classifications are similar, as they classify real and unreal conditionals and direct and indirect conditionals based on the relationship between the main and subordinate clauses in terms of content. The relationship between the main and subordinate clauses in real and direct conditionals is closer than that in unreal and indirect conditionals. However, the third classification is based on whether the situation described in the conditional clause is consistent with reality. In remote conditional constructions, the described situation often differs from reality. Both of these conditional sentence categories can be found in the Companies Ordinance, whose usage and translation will be discussed in detail in Chapter 4.

Currently, *Modern Chinese Descriptive Grammar* (Zhang, 2010) is one of the most authoritative works on Chinese grammar. In this book, complex sentences are classified into three types. (1) The first type is the factual relationship, which refers to the relationship between objective facts, such as coordination and coherence. (2) The second type is the logical relationship, which refers to the relationship between judgements, such as cause and effect, hypothesis, and condition. (3) The third type is the psychological or pragmatic relationship, which relates to the subjective understanding of the speaker, such as progression and contrast (2010: 639).

Zhang (2010) points out that hypothetical complex sentences can be divided into two types: general hypothetical complex sentences and 'otherwise' complex sentences. Since the second type of complex sentence does not appear in the Companies Ordinance, this study focuses on the discussion of the first type. The typical pattern of a general hypothetical complex sentence is 'If p, then q.' Such terms can be used to express hypothesis of '如果' (rú guǒ): 如 (rú), 若 (ruò), 如若 (rú ruò), 若如 (ruò rú), 若是 (ruò shì), 若不然 (ruò bù rán), 要是 (yào shi), 要 (yào), 要不然 (yào bù rán), 假若 (jiǎ ruò), 假使 (jiǎ shǐ), 假如 (jiǎ rú), 假定 (jiǎ dìng), 倘 (tǎng), 倘如 (tǎng rú), 倘若 (tǎng ruò), 倘使 (tǎng shǐ), 倘不然 (tǎng bù rán), 設使 (shè shǐ), 設若 (shè ruò), 設或 (shè huò), and 萬一 (wàn yī). '就' (jiù) can be replaced by '便' (biàn) or 則 (zé), before which '那' (nà) or '那麼 ' (nà me) can be used. It is worth noting that conditional clauses in this book refer to hypothetical complex sentences, rather than conditional complex sentences. One of the typical patterns of conditional complex sentences in Chinese is: '只要 (zhǐ yào; as long as) p, 就 (jiù; then) q.' The difference between the two lies in '如果' (rú guǒ) emphasises subjunctivity while '只要' (zhǐ yào) emphasises conditions—the minimum condition (Zhang, 2010: 678).

In addition, Xu (2002) extensively discusses conditional sentences, pointing out that in Chinese, the sentence pattern 'If p, then q' is the most typical pattern for expressing a hypothetical relationship between clauses. The basic structure of this pattern includes three parts: a hypothetical clause p, a result clause q, and a conjunction connecting them. The semantic characteristics of this pattern mainly manifest as subjunctivity and conditionality. Subjunctivity focuses on the relationship between the situation described in each clause and objective reality. The subjunctivity of the 'If p, then q' pattern is reflected in the fact that both the hypothetical clause and the result clause may or may not represent real situations in the actual world. That is to say, the situation described in either clause may be true in the real world (possibility hypothesis), or it may be the opposite of what actually exists in the real world (counterfactual hypothesis) (Xu, 2002: 23).

The conditionality of this pattern is based on subjunctivity, or in other words, subjunctivity serves the purpose of establishing a condition. Subjunctivity is a phenomenon or a way of constructing a possible world. The formation of any accepted 'If p, then q' construction implies that the speaker has created a possible world that can be accepted by people. In this specific possible world, the existence of p is expected to lead to or result in the occurrence of q. Therefore, in the 'If p, then q' pattern, the speaker constructs a possible world with the purpose of establishing a conditional relationship between the clauses p and q (Xu, 2002: 24).

2.2.2 Status quo of conditional clauses in legal documents

In common texts, although conditional clauses are often introduced by 'if,' there are also other expressions, demonstrating the richness of language. This feature of conditional clauses is also evident in legal language, because legal language shares common features with common texts, serving as the foundation for the correct understanding of legal texts. However, compared with common texts, conditional clauses in legal English possess the logical structure and characteristics of legislative statements. Such legislative statements typically consist of factual situations and legal statements, with the former generally expressed through conditional clauses and the latter through main clauses. The two together form a complete sentence and reflect the rigorous legal logic (Yin & Han, 2009).

Nevertheless, the conditional meaning in legal logic does not entirely rely on the conjunction 'if.' In English, some conjunctions are rarely used to indicate conditional relationships in common texts but are frequently employed in legal texts. For example, the conjunction 'when' predominantly denotes temporal relationships in common texts. But this concept in legal language is often extended to convey a conditional meaning, emphasising the logical relationship between factual situations and legal assertions. There is limited research on conditional clauses in legal texts: Tang's (2010) descriptive translation study of conditional clauses in maritime conventions is the only research identified. Tang believes that the majority of conditional clauses are rendered through hypotactic translation. Although his study provides a comprehensive statistical and descriptive analysis of translation methods for introductory words for conditional clauses, in-depth analysis and explanation are not offered.

Therefore, the current research on conditional clauses is far from sufficient. This study, by exploring the translation of conditional clauses in the Companies Ordinance, aims to identify various translations of introductory words for conditional clauses, highlight the similarities and differences among these introductory words, and examine translation patterns for conditional sentences.

2.2.3 Translation of conditional clauses in legal texts

Regarding the translation of conditional clauses in legal texts, several scholars have presented their own insights. For instance, based on his research on legal texts, Li (2008) employs the method of operative analysis and identifies three main elements in typical legal sentence patterns: legal subject, legal action, and legal case/condition. He argues that procedural legal sentences consist of two basic components: the main clause of legal subject and legal action, and the conditional clause that establishes conditions, qualifications, or requirements. Li summarises the translations of six groups of eight introductory words for conditional clauses commonly found in legal texts. 'If' is generally translated as '如' (rú) or '如果' (rú guǒ) (however, at the national level, abbreviated forms, such as '如' (rú), are seldom used, reflecting the rigorous or conservative nature of legislative language). 'Where' is translated as '凡' (fán) in Hong Kong, while in mainland China, it is commonly expressed by the structure of '……的' (……de). For conditional clauses introduced by 'when,' it is necessary to first determine if it introduces a conditional clause. If so, it can be translated as '如' (rú) or '凡' (fán). 'In case' and 'in the event' are often translated as '萬一' (wàn yī) or '一旦' (yī dàn) to convey the sense of rare occurrences. 'Should' indicates a stronger hypothetical state, and it can be translated as '假如' (jiǎ rú) or '萬一' (wàn yī). 'Provided that' and 'providing that' are archaic terms that can be translated as '倘若' (tǎng ruò), which stylistically pairs well with these archaic terms.

In addition, many scholars, when discussing the translation of long sentences in legal texts, also mention the translation of conditional clauses. Given that legal language tends to be complex, one prominent feature of legal language is the frequent use of long sentences, often referred to as the one-paragraph-one-sentence structure by legal drafters and translators. In English and Chinese legal texts, this tendency to use long sentences stems from the legislators' attempt to encompass all relevant information on a specific issue within a single complete sentence, avoiding potential ambiguity that may arise from several fragmented sentences. For instance, a legislative statement should consist of three or more main clauses, each main clause being further modified and restricted by several subordinate clauses. In this way, such long sentences are less prone to be misunderstood because readers do not need to interpret or verify the relationships between independent sentences. Moreover, a series of short sentences can lead to unnecessary repetition or confusing referential relationships, potentially affecting the effectiveness of communication. Therefore, most scholars advocate for the use of the one-paragraph-one-sentence structure in the drafting and translation of legal texts.

Yuan (2008) points out that due to the normative function and informational function inherent in legal language, which are achieved through prescriptive and descriptive means, the use of conditional clause structures in legal language has become very common. The extensive use of conditional clauses in legal English has long been noticed. Coode (1848) proposed that the elements constituting conditional clauses in legal English can be categorised as case, condition, legal subject, and legal action. Coode firstly explains the two essential elements of the legal subject and the legal action (Coode, 1848: 9–10):

> The person who may or may not, or shall or shall not do something or submit to something, is the legal subject of the legal action … The description of the legal subject determines the extent of the law. On this portion of every legal sentence it depends whether a right or privilege shall be limited to too few persons or extended to too many; whether an obligation is imposed on more persons than is necessary or is not extended to sufficient persons in order to secure the correlative right; whether powers are reposed in right or wrong persons; whether sanctions are or are not made to fall on the proper subjects. Generally, be the law in itself good or bad, it is on this portion, the description of the legal subject, that its equal or unequal incidence upon persons depends … The legal action is that part of every legislative sentence in which the right, privilege, or power, or the obligation or liability, is defined, wherein it is said that a person may or may not, or shall or shall not do any act, or shall submit to some act. As the legal subject defines the extent of the law, so the description of the legal action expresses the nature of the law. The selection of the legal subject is important; but it is on the description of the legal action that the whole function of legislation exercises and exhausts itself … Such are the essential elements of every legal sentence. Without both the legal subject and the legal action no law can be written; and all enactments of universal and constant operation consist of these alone.

Then Coode continues to explain the optional elements of the case and the condition (Coode, 1848: 22–23):

> It is, that wherever the law is intended to operate only in certain circumstances, those circumstances should be invariably described before any other part of the enactment is expressed … A law universal as to its subjects, and restricted or not restricted to certain occasions (cases), may still operate only upon the performance by some person of certain conditions. It is not till something has been done that the right can be enjoyed, or that compliance with the obligation can be enforced, or that the liability can be applied. These conditions are invariably conditions precedent. The action of the law never takes place till these are complied with. No such thing as the so-called conditions subsequent or executory can be conceived to apply to a legal action. The expression of the condition is of very high importance … Conditions are more frequently expressed as the conditions of enforcing an obligation on another; if in these cases the condition is in any respect more stringent than necessary, it so far prevents the enforcement of the obligation; on the other hand, every word by which the condition is made less stringent makes the obligation more so, and renders the law unnecessarily hard, by imposing

> obligations of an extent disproportionate to the value of the right to which they subserve.

He mentioned several examples to explain those four elements, and two typical examples are presented here (Coode, 1848: 39):

> Example 1:
>
> Legal case: Where any Quaker refuses to pay any church rates,
> Legal condition: if any churchwarden complains thereof,
> Legal subject: one of the next Justices of the peace,
> Legal action: may summon such Quaker.

In this example, the first two components are used to describe the legal case and the legal condition, while the latter two components are used to describe the legal subject and the legal action they should take.

> Example 2:
>
> Cases: Where there is any question between any 'parishes' touching the boundaries of such 'parishes',
> or where such parishes are desirous of having such boundaries ascertained, or a new boundary line defined;
> Condition: if a majority of not less than two-thirds in number and value of the landowners of such parishes make application in writing;
> Legal subject: THE TITHE COMMISSIONERS for England and Wales, or any of their Assistant Commissioners,
> First legal action: may deal with any dispute or question concerning such boundaries,
> Second legal action: and may ascertain, adjust, set out, and define the ancient boundaries between such parishes,
> Third legal action: or may draw and define a new line of boundary as they may see fit.

In this example, longer and more complicated than Example 1, there are two legal cases, one legal condition, one legal subject, and three legal actions. As long as we identify those four elements, we can clearly understand the sentence structure.

In English legal provisions, the fact situation is typically expressed by a conditional clause, while the statement of law is expressed by the main clause. Together, they form a complete sentence that conveys the legal logic structure of 'If P1 + P2, then Q.' Therefore, Coode's Example 1 can be rewritten in the following form:

> Fact-situation: where a churchwarden files a complaint against a Quaker for refusing to pay any church rates
> Statement of law: one of the next Justices of the peace may summon such Quaker

In legal translation, it is essential for translators to grasp the feature of conditional clauses. Conditional clauses in legal English are often expressed in the following formula: 'If X, then Y shall do Z' or 'If X, then Y shall be Z.' Here, 'If X' represents the case to which the legal system applies, 'Y' represents the legal subject, and 'Z' represents the legal action. This format is widely used in legal English, and understanding this format is helpful for translating conditional clauses.

2.3 Research gap

Given the status quo of the above research, there is still significant research space with regard to conditional clauses in legal texts and further investigation can be conducted on the specific analysis of such sentences. Therefore, the author has chosen the Companies Ordinance as the research subject to examine different translations of conditional clauses. The selection of Hong Kong ordinances is based on the following four reasons:

(1) Firstly, Hong Kong is a bilingual society, and its legal system requires the availability of both Chinese and English versions of ordinances, which are equally authentic. This provides a complete parallel text for the analysis of conditional clauses in this study.
(2) Secondly, conditional clauses are important syntactic structures in legislative provisions, and according to the author's preliminary statistics, conditional clauses have a significant presence in Hong Kong legislation (e.g., accounting for 44% in the Companies Ordinance). Therefore, gaining an in-depth understanding of the syntactic structure and translation patterns of conditional clauses is of great significance.
(3) Thirdly, the derived translation patterns can serve as reference guidelines for translators in handling the translation of conditional clauses in the future.
(4) Lastly, there are relatively few scholars who have conducted comprehensive research on Hong Kong bilingual ordinances, particularly on sentence structures (or more specifically, conditional clauses). Hence, exploring various translations and patterns for conditional clauses in this context would greatly assist translators in effectively translating legal texts.

2.4 Summary

This chapter primarily examines the existing literature in legal translation research, categorising the research achievements into four aspects: translation of legal terms, features of legal language, theories, principles, and methods of legal translation, as well as research on legal text types and other related areas. It can be observed that significant progress has been made in these areas of legal translation research; however, the study of sentence structures in legal texts, particularly the analysis of conditional clauses, is relatively insufficient. Then the chapter summarises the research on sentence structures in legal texts, with a specific focus on the study of conditional clauses. Also, the chapter highlights the differences in the use of conditional clauses between general texts and legal texts, identifies the syntactic characteristics of conditional clauses in legal texts, and explores their translation patterns. It is evident that there is ample research space for exploring the translation of conditional clauses through detailed analysis. Subsequently, this book attempts to investigate the various translation methods and sentence patterns of conditional clauses in the context of the Companies Ordinance, in order to provide references for translators when translating conditional clauses.

References

Alcaraz Varó, Enrique & Hughes, Brain. *Legal Translation Explained.* Manchester; Northampton: St. Jerome Publishing, 2002.

Bhatia, Vijay K. *Analysing Genre—Language Use in Professional Settings.* New York: Longman Group Limited, 1993.

Cao, Deborah. *Translating Law*. Clevedon; Buffalo: Multilingual Matters, 2007.

Carter, Ronald & McCarthy, Michael. *Cambridge Grammar of English: A Comprehensive Guide – Spoken and Written English Grammar and Usage*. Cambridge: Cambridge University Press, 2006.

Coode, George. *On Legislative Expression; or, The Language of the Written Law.* Introduction to a digest of the Poor Laws attached to the 1843 Report of the Poor Law Commission. Repr. In Drieger, E.A. (1957), The Composition of Legislation, 1848.

Gibbons, John. *Forensic Linguistics: An Introduction to Language in the Justice System.* Malden, MA: Blackwell Publishing, 2003.

Huddleston, Rodney & Pullum Geoffrey K. *The Cambridge Grammar of the English Language*. Cambridge: Cambridge University Press, 2002.

Mellinkoff, David. *The Language of the Law*. Boston: Little, Brown and Company, 1990.

Palmer, F.R. *The English Verb*. London: Longman Group Limited, 1974.

Quirk, Randolph, Greenbaum, Sidney, Leech, Geoffrey, & Svartvik, Jan *A Comprehensive Grammar of the English Language*. London; New York: Longman, 1985.

Šarčević, Susan. *New Approach to Legal Translation.* The Hague; Boston: Kluwer Law International, 1997.

Chen, Jiangping [陳建平]. 法律文體翻譯探索 [*An Exploration into the Translation of Legal Texts*]. 杭州：浙江大學出版社 [Hangzhou: Zhejiang University Press], 2007.

Chen, Zhongcheng [陳忠誠]. 法窗譯話 [*Translating Legal Language*]. 北京：中國對外翻譯出版公司 [Beijing: China Translation & Publishing Corporation], 1998.

Chen, Zhongcheng [陳忠誠].法苑譯譚 [*Translation Talks in the Legal Garden*]. 北京：中國法制出版社 [Beijing: China Legal Publishing House], 2000.

Du, Jinbang [杜金榜]. 法律語言學 [*Forensic Linguistics*]. 上海：上海外語教育出版社 [Shanghai: Shanghai Foreign Language Education Press], 2004.

Du, Jinbang, Zhang, Fu, & Yuan, Liang [杜金榜、張福、袁亮]. 中國法律法規英譯的問題和解決 [Problems and solutions to the English translation of Chinese laws and regulations]. 中國翻譯 [*Chinese Translators Journal*], 2004(3): 72–76.

Fu, Weiliang [傅偉良]. 合同法律文件翻譯談—談《中華人民共和國合同法》的部分譯文 [Talk on translation of legal documents and contract documents – Commenting on parts of English version of the translation of the contract law of people's Republic of China]. 中國翻譯 [*Chinese Translators Journal*], 2002 (5): 42–45.

Ji, Yiguang [季益廣]. 法律英語的文體特點及英譯技巧 [Stylistic characteristics of legal English and English translation skills]. 中國翻譯 [*Chinese Translators Journal*], 1999 (4): 6–9.
Li, Kexing [李克興]. 論法律翻譯的基本原則 [On basic principles of legal translation]. 翻譯季刊 [*Translation Quarterly*], 1997 (3&4): 176–201.
Li, Kexing [李克興]. 法律翻譯理論與實踐 [*Legal Translation: A Theoretical and Practical Approach*]. 北京：北京大學出版社 [Beijing: Peking University Press]. 2007.
Li, Kexing [李克興]. 法律英語條件句的寫作和翻譯 [Composing and translating conditional clauses in legal texts]. 中國翻譯 [*Chinese Translators Journal*], 2008 (4)：71–77, 96.
Lin, Kenan & Ji, Mingwen [林克難、籍明文]. 法律文字中‘的’字结构翻译探讨. 中國科技翻譯 [*Chinese Science & Technology Translators Journal*], 2002 (3): 20–22.
Li, Li [李麗]. 法律英語詞彙的特點及其翻譯 [Lexical characteristics of legal English and the translation] 中國科技翻譯 [*Chinese Science & Technology Translators Journal*], 2005 (3): 14–16.
Qiu, Guixi [邱貴溪]. 論法律文件翻譯的若干原則 [Some principles for the translation of documents of law]. 中國科技翻譯 [*Chinese Science & Technology Translators Journal*], 2000 (2): 14–17.
Qu, Wensheng & Xing, Caixia [屈文生、邢彩霞]. "法律翻譯中的"條"、"款"、"項"、"目" ["article", "paragraph", "subparagraph", and "item" in legal translation]. 中國翻譯 [*Chinese Translators Journal*], 2005 (2): 63–66.
Sun, Wanbiao [孫萬彪]. 漢英法律翻譯教程[*A Course in Translation of Legal Documents: Chinese-English*]. 上海：上海外語教育出版社 [Shanghai: Shanghai Foreign Language Education Press], 2004.
Sun, Wanbiao [孫萬彪]. 英漢法法律翻譯教程[*A Course in Translation of Legal Documents: English-Chinese*]. 上海：上海外語教育出版社 [Shanghai: Shanghai Foreign Language Education Press], 2003.
Tang, Peipei [唐培培]. 基於語料庫的國際海事公約中條件句翻譯的描述性研究 [*A Corpus-based Descriptive Study on the Translation of Conditionals in International Maritime Conventions*]. 大連海事大學 [Dalian Maritime University], Master dissertation in 2010.
Wang, Daogeng [王道庚]. 法律翻譯：理論與實踐 [*Legal Translation – Theory and Practice*]. 香港：香港城市大學出版社 [Hong Kong: City University of Hong Kong Press], 2006.
Wang, Jian [王建]. 影響法律英語翻譯的因素 [On the factors that influence the translation of legal English]. 中國科技翻譯 [*Chinese Science & Technology Translators Journal*], 2003 (1): 1–5.
Xiao, Yunshu [肖雲樞]. 英漢法律術語的特點、詞源及翻譯 [The Characteristics, etymology and translation of legal terms both in English and Chinese]. 中國翻譯 [Chinese Translators Journal], 2001 (3): 44–47.
Xin, Gu [辛谷]. 法律法規名稱的翻譯 [Translation of names of laws and regulations]. 中國科技翻譯 [*Chinese Science & Technology Translators Journal*], 2003 (3): 25–28.
Xu, Lijie [徐李潔]. IF-條件句分類再研究 [Reinvestigating categories of IF-conditional clauses]. 四川外語學院學報 [*Journal of Sichuan International Studies University*], 2005 (2): 64–69.
Xu, Yangchun [徐陽春]. 現代漢語複句的各種類型 [*A Study on Sentence Patterns of Modern Chinese Complex Sentences*]. 北京：中國社會科學出版社 [Beijing: China Social Sciences Press], 2002.

Yin, Hongshan & Han, Yuhua [尹洪山、韓玉花]. 立法語言中的條件概念及其翻譯技巧 [Conditional concept in legislative language and the translation thereof]. 青島科技大學學報 [*The Journal of Qingdao University of Science and Technology*], 2009 (4): 92–94.

Yuan, Huaping [袁華平]. 法律英語中長句的翻譯 [Translation of long sentences in legal English]. 湖南農業大學學報 [*Journal of Hunan Agricultural University*], 2008 (6): 147–149.

Zhang, Bin [張斌]. 現代漢語描寫語法 [*Modern Chinese Descriptive Grammar*]. 北京：商務印書館 [Beijing: The Commercial Press], 2010.

Zhang, Zhenbang [章振邦].新編英語語法教程 [*A New English Grammar Coursebook*]. 上海：上海外語教育出版社 [Shanghai: Shanghai Foreign Language Education Press], 1989.

Zhu, Dingchu [朱定初]. 評復旦大學《法律英語》中的譯註—兼談法律專門術語翻譯的基本原則 [Comments on the mistranslated terms in English for the legal profession: Some basic rules of translation of legal terms of art]. 中國翻譯 [*Chinese Translators Journal*], 2002 (3): 65–70.

3 Text typology and legal translation

3.1 Text typology in translation studies

There are two types of classification of text types based on different standards: the first one is the early classification based on the subject matter, and the second one is the classification proposed by Reiss, which categorises texts according to their functions.

3.1.1 Classification based on the subject matter

Classification based on the subject matter refers to categorising texts according to the specific subject or content they address.

(1) Translation of biblical texts and non-biblical texts

The translation of biblical texts can be traced back to as early as 340 AD when Hieronymus, i.e., Saint Jerome, one of the most influential translation theorists in Western history and the official translator of the Bible, stated that,

> Now I not only admit but freely announce that in translating from the Greek - except of course in the case of Holy Scripture, where even the syntax contains a mystery - I render, not word for word, but sense for sense.
> (cited in Robinson, 1997: 25)

During that time, the Bible was considered supremely sacred and inviolable for Christians, and not everyone could interpret it. Translators of the Bible had to hold a high position and were required to provide a literal translation of its content without arbitrary interpretations or alternations. Based on this, Hieronymus classified texts into biblical texts and non-biblical texts and believed that the translation of the Bible should be word for word, while non-biblical texts should be sense for sense.

(2) Translation of literary texts and non-literary texts

From the 14th century, Europe witnessed the Renaissance movement, which advocated for individual liberation, opposed medieval religious beliefs, and challenged the intellectual constraints imposed by the Church. It affirmed human rights, rejected divine authority, and cast aside the authority of theology and traditional dogmas. The Renaissance movement had a profound impact on various fields,

DOI: 10.4324/9781003359180-3

including natural sciences, painting, music, literature, architecture, and more. With the increased status of literature, the translation of literary texts gradually gained recognition and attention. Therefore, texts are classified into literary and non-literary categories. Even today, many scholars follow this classification, and numerous translation researchers invest their efforts in the study of literary translation.

(3) Translation of artistic works and commercial texts

In the early 19th century, Schleiermacher limited his research to translation from one language into another, and he proposed two types of translation: translation in the field of commerce and translation in the fields of scholarship and art. He also pointed out that there is no absolute boundary between these two types of translation, which overlap to some extent (cited in Robinson, 1997: 226). He referred to the first type of translation as the work of an interpreter, where oral communication is paramount in the commercial field. The second type of translation is the responsibility of the translator proper, as only written translation can ensure the longevity of artistic and scholarly works.

(4) Translation of texts with conceptual and interpersonal functions

House is one of the scholars who applied Halliday's systemic functional linguistics to translation studies. Based on the framework of functional linguistics, she proposed a quality assessment system for translation. Regarding text types, she believed that Reiss's and Vermeer's classification of text types was too simple, though it can serve as a basis for selecting and categorising texts for analysis. Instead, by adopting a traditional two-fold classification and labelling it with the functional linguistic terms 'ideational' and 'interpersonal,' House divided translation into two categories: conceptual function and interpersonal function. The conceptual function is further divided into technical texts and non-technical texts, while the interpersonal function is divided into fictional and non-fictional texts (House, 1997: 36).

(5) Translation of practical texts and literary or artistic texts

Delisle believed that translation is a complex task and that the translation process cannot be simplified. Regardless of the nature of the text to be translated, different requirements are placed on the translator's qualifications. Some texts require the translator to have a command of specific language registers and a keen artistic sense (such as literary texts), while others require the translator to possess specialised knowledge (such as technical and scientific texts). Dennis focused more on the translation of practical and ordinary texts. He pointed out that his research is limited to pragmatic texts, thereby excluding the study of literary texts, and he believed that these two types of texts have different characteristics. It can be seen that he divided translation into two categories: pragmatic texts and literary or artistic texts (Delisle, 1988: 1).

(6) Translation of literary texts, general language texts, and special language texts

Snell-Hornby put forward a prototypology for different types of text translation and provided a blueprint for various types of text translation. She adopted an integrated approach to text classification and established translation models for each text type, so as to determine translation standards based on the characteristics of each text type. She categorised texts into three types: literary translation, general language translation, and special language translation. In her prototypology, Snell-Hornby classified legal texts as a category of special language texts (Snell-Hornby, 1988: 32). Furthermore, she emphasised that these classifications are not fixed but a dynamic continuum, reflecting the dynamic relationship between text types and translation criteria.

(7) Literary translation, Bible translation, and industrial translation

Sager classified translation activities into three types: literary translation, Bible translation, and industrial translation. Specifically,

> Literary translation is generally considered somehow different from other translations and we instinctively put it into a separate category. This is largely because the purpose of a literary work cannot be specified in the simple terms of the intentions hitherto presented; nor can reader expectation be so analysed ... Bible translation has historically been perceived as a separate form with its own methods and practices justified by the nature of the source language texts, the historical distance between text and reader, the inherent value and integrity of the texts as a whole and, of course, the use of these texts ... The third major translation activity is much less coherent and embraces all professional translation outside these two areas. They are grouped together here as a basis for establishing a model of the translation process which accounts for the regular application of machine translation and other advanced tools of the language industry.
>
> (Sager, 1993: 160–165)

From the above seven classifications of texts, it can be seen that legal texts hold a distinct position among all texts. The translation of legal texts differs from the translation of literary or artistic works. It falls under the category of non-literary, practical, industrial, commercial texts, or special texts. This viewpoint is widely shared among scholars. However, there are certain flaws in using the classification based on subject matter to determine the translation strategy for legal translation. Firstly, some scholars (e.g., Schleiermacher) argue that the translation of commercial texts (including legal texts) can be achieved through interlingual substitution. They believe that the meaning and expression of such texts are essentially the same across different languages. Consequently, the translation of these texts requires neither interpretation nor artistic creativity. It is viewed as a mechanical process and thus an inferior type of translation. Clearly, this perspective is one-sided. Nowadays, legal translators are required not only to master two or more languages but also to possess in-depth knowledge of various legal concepts, legal systems, and other specialised expertise. Legal translation is far from being a mechanical process, and labelling it as 'inferior translation' is unfounded. Secondly, this kind of broad classification fails to assist in determining the translation strategies for specific texts. While this classification can determine the category to which legal texts belong, it does not provide specific translation strategies for a particular text type, such as legal texts. Therefore, an alternative classification method is needed to differentiate the categories of legal texts in detail and thus determine appropriate translation strategies for legal texts.

3.1.2 Classification based on text function

With the emergence of sociolinguistics, pragmatics, and functional linguistics, some scholars have recognised the importance of language function and have attempted to classify translated texts based on their language functions. While the traditional classification of texts mentioned earlier is too general, it can be said that Reiss's text typology provides a more systematic and scientifically grounded approach, with greater practical value. According to the traditional classification, legal texts are considered of low translation status, and the translation strategy should be literal translation. However, these arguments, which are mainly based on the nature of legal texts themselves and the characteristics of legal language, overlook a crucial point: legal translation, the same as other texts, serves a function. Reiss's text typology provides a new framework for legal translation by asserting that different types of texts have different functions, and it is the function that determines the text type. Nevertheless, scholars still hold divergent views on the functions of legal texts within the framework of translation typology. By examining different scholars' perspectives on the functions of legal texts, this study aims to explore the primary functions of legal texts.

In the 1970s, the German scholar Reiss introduced functionalism, which had a significant influence on the development of contemporary translation theories. Functionalism, further developed by subsequent scholars such as Nord, Vermeer, Snell-Hornby, and House, formed an important school known as German functionalism. The main members of this school are still active in the translation arena today. Reiss's major contribution to translation theories was the introduction of text typology within the framework of functionalism, i.e., different types of texts require different translation strategies. In the past, scholars attempted to establish a translation strategy applicable to all texts. However, Reiss broke away from this framework and put forward the innovative concept that different texts serve different functions, and these functions determine the text type, which in turn determines its translation strategy.

Many scholars have explored the functions of legal translation. For example:

(1) Jumpelt categorised special-purpose texts into four groups based on disciplines: technical texts, texts of the natural sciences, texts of the social sciences, and other texts. The category of texts of the social sciences includes sociology, economics, political science, finance, and law. Jumpelt argues that all special-purpose texts serve the function of providing information and have an informative function (cited in Šarčević, 1997). In other words, Jumpelt suggests that legal texts, including those within the social sciences, are also texts with an informative function.

(2) Reiss (1971) proposed a translation-oriented text typology based not only on the subject matter but, more importantly, on text function. Her text typology was inspired by Bühler's (1990) three-fold classification of language functions, which categorises texts into expressive, conative, and informative functions. In subsequent research, Reiss provided numerous examples to support her findings. Reiss opined that informative texts include notices, reports, philosophical texts, and essays, as well as laws and contracts, which means she classified laws and contracts as informative texts, the same as Jumpelt's perspective.
(3) Weber demonstrated that the formal linguistic characteristics of special-purpose texts are determined by their functions. He proposed a typology for creating special-purpose texts based on Halliday's functional types. According to Weber, texts can be predominantly instrumental, regulatory, interactional, personal, heuristic, imaginative, or representational. However, his analysis indicates that special-purpose texts have only one function, which is representational. This finding supports the notion that special-purpose texts, including legal texts, primarily serve an informative function (cited in Šarčević, 1997).
(4) Newmark also classified texts based on Bühler's model of language functions. However, unlike Reiss, Newmark recognised that while statutes and contracts can be considered informative to some extent, their primary function is not to provide information but rather to make appeals or give commands. Therefore, Newmark categorised statutes as vocative texts, which serve a vocative function. Furthermore, he distinguished this function into two subcategories: directive and imperative (Newmark, 1982: 13–15). Later, he expanded the classification by incorporating Jacobson's theory and added aesthetic, phatic, and metalingual functions. However, Newmark changed his previous view and categorised regulations and legal texts as expressive texts, considering the core of expressive function to be the thoughts of the speaker or author. Thus, laws and regulations are seen as authoritative texts under the category of expressive texts. Newmark's expressive texts include serious imaginative literature, authoritative statements, autobiography, essays, and personal correspondence. When discussing authoritative statements, he mentioned statutes and legal documents, suggesting that they belong to expressive texts along with serious literature, autobiography, essays, and personal correspondence (Newmark, 1988: 39).
(5) Sager proposed five purposes of communication: social, informative, directive, discursive, and evaluative. He emphasised that

> Directive messages are reader-oriented: if readers respond in the expected way, or more specifically, do what they have been told, the communication has been successful ... The most basic example of the directive purpose is seen in requests, orders, instructions, prohibitions, exhortations, warnings and their distinctive formal requirements are obvious ... The directive purpose may apply to a limited number of readers only, as in laws and regulations where the purpose is

> informative for the general reader and directive for the specific group of people listed, or falling into the categories set out.
>
> (Sager, 1993: 70)

(6) Jiang (1995: 211–213) based his analysis on Nida's (1964) eight functions of language communication: expressive function, cognitive function, interpersonal function, informative function, directive function, operative function, emotive function, and aesthetic function. By excluding certain functions, Jiang identified the primary functions of legal discourse. He argued that the emotive and aesthetic functions are exclusive to literary discourse and have no relevance to legal discourse. The expressive and interpersonal functions primarily belong to conversational discourse. The cognitive function mainly pertains to scientific and political discourse and is less relevant to legal discourse. Therefore, the remaining three functions, namely informative, directive, and operative functions, are the key functions of legal discourse. Jiang (1995: 213) further pointed out,

> As the carrier of legal information, the first function of legal discourse is to bear, store, transmit, and convey legal information, which is the informative function of legal discourse ... Another important function of legal discourse is issuing directives because legal discourse is not just general information but a type of directive information ... Its content instructs people to engage in lawful behaviour and prohibits them from engaging in unlawful behaviour, thereby regulating social behaviour ... The third function of legal discourse is the execution of laws and orders as a tool for law enforcement, which is its operative function.

(7) Teng and Kong (2008: 38) discussed the text types of legal texts. They criticised the tendency of some scholars (including Reiss) to categorise the main functions of legal texts as either informative or vocative and argued that such categorisation overlooks the holistic picture. They proposed that the primary function of prescriptive legal texts is to provide accurate information to readers about rights, obligations, and restrictions, and the function of non-prescriptive legal texts is focused on presenting the case instead of purely conveying information. They fully agree with Snell-Hornby's viewpoint that the translation of legal documents should be considered a form of special language translation that prioritises textual information (Snell-Hornby, 1988: 32).

(8) Jürgen Habermas, a philosopher and sociologist, agrees with Bühler's classification and undoubtedly asserts that laws and contracts have a regulatory function, belonging to the category of vocative texts in Bühler's classification (cited in Šarčević, 1997).

(9) Šarčević argued that the primary function of legal texts is not only to provide information but, more importantly, to have a vocative function. She believed that the core of legal translation is to express the same intention as the original text, rather than its content or form. She revisited Bühler's three-fold

classification of language functions, namely informative function (primarily describing the state of the real world, emphasising the text of objects and/or facts), expressive function (sender-oriented, aiming to enrich the world), and vocative function (receiver-oriented, aiming to change the world by inspiring or imposing behaviour on the receiver). From the examples cited by Bühler, Šarčević observed that the vocative texts not only include persuasive texts but also regulatory texts. It is evident that laws and regulations belong to the category of regulatory texts. Although Bühler did not specifically mention legal texts, he emphasised that texts controlled by imperative sentences fall into the category of vocative texts, and imperative sentences are frequently used in regulatory texts. Therefore, Šarčević classified legal texts as a type of vocative text (1997: 10). Based on this, she put forward her own viewpoint (Šarčević, 1997: 73):

> The (legal) translator's main task is to produce a text that will lead to the same legal effects in practice … While the presumption of equal effect has priority over that of equal meaning, both are subordinate to the presumption of equal intent.

Based on the above analysis of different scholars' perspectives, it is undeniable that there is a trend to classify texts based on their functions (such as Sager). However, there are inconsistent views among scholars regarding the functions of legal texts. In the following analysis, a detailed examination will be conducted, so as to identify the text types of legal texts and corresponding translation strategies.

3.2 Text typology in legal translation

The aforementioned scholars have put forward their own views on the types of legal texts, which can be broadly categorised into three groups.

(1) The first group, represented by Jumpelt, Reiss, and Weber, considers legal texts as informative texts. They approach legal texts from the perspective of the source text, i.e., focusing on the content of the legal text itself, and they argue that their main function is to provide information. From this viewpoint, legal texts are seen as informative texts. For example, when Chinese people read legal provisions from Western countries, they are primarily concerned with understanding the content of the legal provisions. Therefore, from this perspective, legal texts are considered informative texts.
(2) The second group, represented by Newmark, views legal texts as expressive texts. They approach legal texts from the standpoint of the author of the original text, examining the author's viewpoints, attitudes, and other factors behind the content of the legal text. From this perspective, legal texts are seen as expressive, whose primary function is no longer to provide information but to reflect the original author's stance or attitude.

(3) The third group, represented by Habermas, Bühler, and Šarčević, argues that legal texts are vocative texts. This perspective focuses on the reader of the translated text and emphasises that the intention is the core and the main function is to convey the same intention as the original text. The premise of this viewpoint is that the translated text has the same legal effect as the source text, such as in the case of Hong Kong. However, this perspective only applies when the function of the translated text is consistent with the function of the source text and overlooks the case when the functions of the translated text and the source text may differ.

In order to clarify the terms 'function' and 'intention,' which have been used by scholars such as Šarčević, it is important to provide detailed explanations. Nord distinguishes between the two: 'function refers to what a text means or is intended to mean from the receiver's point of view';

> intention is defined from the viewpoint of the sender, who wants to achieve a certain purpose with the text. Yet the best of intentions do not guarantee a perfect result, particularly in cases where the situations of the sender and the receiver differ considerably. In accordance with the model of text-bound interaction, the receivers use the text with a certain function, depending on their own expectations, needs, previous knowledge and situational conditions. In an ideal situation, the sender's intention will find its aim, in which case intention and function would be analogous or even identical.
>
> (Nord, 1997: 28)

As far as this study is concerned, there is no fundamental difference between the function and intention of the text. The key issue lies not in the difference between the terms 'function' and 'intention,' but in the discrepancies between the function or intention of the translated text and the source text. Therefore, Nord's viewpoint can be revised as follows: the function (or intention) of the translated text may differ from the function (or intention) of the source text, and they are only consistent in ideal circumstances. This theoretical foundation supports the proposition in this book, which differentiates between two cases when categorising legal text types.

The viewpoints of the scholars mentioned above, contradictory as they are, are all correct and valid because they discuss different cases of legal text translation. Based on this, two cases should be taken into account for determining the text types of legal texts: (1) When the function of the translated text is consistent with the function of the source text, i.e., the translated text has the same legal effect as the source text in the target language, then the translated text can be considered as vocative. In this case, the focus is on the reader of the translated text, and the function becomes the most important aspect. (2) When the function of the translated text differs from the function of the source text, e.g., the translated text does not have legal effect in the target language, then the translated text can be either informative (based on the content of the source text) or expressive (based on the perspective of the original author).

Examples are provided to illustrate these two cases:

> Example 1: if a Western country were to translate the *Great Qing Legal Code* from Chinese into English, the translated text would obviously not have legal effect. There are two possible interpretations: (1) The Western readers would translate the text to understand the content of the legal provisions in the *Great Qing Legal Code*. In this case, the function of the translated text would be informative, making it an informative text type. This differs from the original function of the *Great Qing Legal Code*, i.e., there is an inconsistency between the function of the translated text and the source text. (2) The readers would study the content of the *Great Qing Legal Code* to gain insights into the historical and cultural context of China at that time and understand certain viewpoints or attitudes of the authors. From this perspective, the function of the translated text would go beyond providing information.
>
> Example 2: after China's joining the World Trade Organization (WTO), it is necessary to have an understanding of global laws and regulations. For instance, if China were to translate American legal provisions into Chinese, the translated text would clearly have no legal effect in China but would primarily serve the purpose of providing information to help Chinese readers better understand the content of American legal provisions. Therefore, the function of the translated text would be different from the function of the source text.
>
> Example 3: in Hong Kong, where bilingual legislation is implemented, the function of the translated text is consistent with the function of the source text. This is because the source text and the translated text (or bilingual texts) have equal legal effects and are equally authentic. In this case, the text type of the legal text is undoubtedly vocative, sharing the same function as the source text. Therefore, the function becomes the primary consideration.

Based on these three examples, it becomes clear that the text type of legal texts should be determined based on whether the translated text has legal effects in the target language. The scholars mentioned earlier failed to recognise the need to differentiate between these two cases when categorising legal text types and overlooked one of the two cases, thus drawing incomplete conclusions. The most important point is that they did not realise that the function of the source text and the function of the translated text can be different. They did not consider the case when the functions of the source text and the translated text are inconsistent. Therefore, when we determine translation strategies for legal texts, it is crucial to distinguish between these two cases in order to make accurate and comprehensive judgements regarding the text type of legal texts.

In the specific case of Hong Kong's bilingual legislation, it is evident that the bilingual ordinances in Hong Kong have legal effects, and the functions of the original English text and the translated Chinese text are the same. Therefore, the text type of Hong Kong's bilingual legislation is vocative.

3.3 Translation strategies

Based on the text typology of legal texts elaborated in Section 3.2, we are now in a position to discuss translation strategies of legal texts. Several scholars (such as Reiss and Newmark) have explored the relations between text type and translation strategies.

3.3.1 Translation strategies of legal texts

Throughout history, many scholars have discussed the issue of translation strategies, such as literal translation (word-for-word translation) and free translation (meaning-based translation). However, there is no clear boundary between literal and free translation.

> Hence most so-called literal translations are in fact compromises with the ideal: looser renditions that replace individual SL [source language] words with individual TL [target language] words wherever possible, and cling as closely as possible to the SL word order in the TL.
>
> (Robinson in Baker, 1998: 125)

In the translation field, views on translation strategies mainly revolve around the concept of 'equivalence,' attempting to explore the extent to which the translated text should be equivalent to the source text and the aspects in which the translated text is equivalent. However, the root of this issue lies in the difficulty of simultaneously achieving equivalence in both the content and form of the translation. Consequently, two different translation strategies emerged: one emphasises content, while the other emphasises form. Essentially, all translation strategies are based on these two different emphases, the proposed concepts being fundamentally dichotomic.

Numerous concepts and strategies have been proposed, each addressing the relationship between form and content. Some examples include:

- Chinese traditional Buddhist sutra translation and the concept of 'Wen Zhi' (form and content).
- Concepts of literal translation and free translation.
- Yan Fu's 'faithfulness, expressiveness, elegance.'
- Lin Yutang's 'fidelity, fluency, and beauty.'
- Fu Lei's theory of 'vividness' (emphasising the importance of capturing the spirit rather than the form in translation).
- Qian Zhongshu's theory of 'the sublime realm.'
- Lu Xun's perspective of 'faithfulness over smoothness.'
- Nida's concept of formal equivalence and dynamic equivalence (or flexible equivalence and functional equivalence).
- Newmark's semantic translation and communicative translation.
- House's covert translation and overt translation.

- Gutt's direct translation and indirect translation.
- Toury's acceptability and adequacy.
- Venuti's domestication and foreignisation.

All these concepts revolve around the dichotomy of form and content. Scholars have recognised that, in the process of translation, it is often challenging to balance both form and content at the same time, often requiring the sacrifice of one to preserve the other. However, many of these translation theories or strategies were primarily developed for literary translation, and many practical translation scholars believe that they may not be suitable for translating non-literary works. Therefore, specific translation strategies or methods for legal texts are put forward by some scholars. For instance, Li (2010: 62) suggests that the primary function of legal texts is informative, so the translation strategy adopted for legal texts should be static equivalence. He points out that the legal translation strategy has a direct and inevitable relationship with the objectives of the source legal text. The essence of formulating any strategy is ultimately to serve that objective. So the ideal state of a translated version is to convey accurately and completely every intent of the author (legislator or legal drafter) of the source legal text, representing all the information, from quality to quantity to style and format, as fully and accurately as possible. In this way, maximum equivalence between the information in the translated version and the source text can be achieved, enabling the translated version to fulfil the same function as the source legal text and to produce similar legal effects. This is the purpose of legal translation.

According to the theory of translation typology, the translation strategy is determined by the text type. After the analysis of the text type of legal texts, it is crucial for legal translators to determine the appropriate translation strategy based on the text type. Based on Reiss's translation typology, we can conclude that the function of a text determines its type, and the text type determines the translation strategy. Although Reiss did not provide a comprehensive judgement on the function of legal texts, her logical deduction is correct, that is, the text type can determine the translation strategy. Newmark also proposed different translation strategies for different types of texts based on Bühler's language functions. Newmark (1988: 47) believes that expressive texts can be translated by semantic translation strategies, while informative and vocative texts can be translated by communicative translation strategies. He further points out that in the translation of vocative texts, achieving equivalence is more important (1988: 48). Therefore, his translation strategies for the three types are summarised in Table 3.1.

Based on the previous description and discussion, it is important to first distinguish the functions of legal texts in different cases, before the translation strategies for legal translation can be determined.

3.3.2 Translation strategies of Hong Kong bilingual ordinances

According to Šarčević (1997), translating texts within the same legal system is relatively easier as there are fewer inconsistent concepts. However, legal translation

Table 3.1 Newmark's definition of text typology and translation strategies

Text typology	*Core*	*Emphasis*	*Translation strategies*
Expressive	Writer/original text	Form	Semantic translation
Informative	Subject matter/truth	Content	Communicative translation (including dynamic equivalence)
Vocative	Readers/translated text	Function	Communicative translation strategy (with an emphasis on achieving equivalence)

in the Hong Kong context is more complex, as it involves two different legal systems. In the process of translating from English to Chinese, both versions have the same and equal legal effect in society. Therefore, the intention to be conveyed by both versions is the same. That is to say, in the case of translating across two different legal systems, it is crucial for the translated language to follow the legal concepts expressed in the source text, so as to ensure consistency in the intention conveyed by both versions. Therefore, in the translation process, when legal concepts differ from those in the source text, it is necessary to adopt the terminology of the legal concepts used in the source text rather than using concepts from the legal system in the target language, which might lead to misunderstandings. In particular, when encountering legal concepts that do not exist in the target language, the translator has to create new terms in the translation to avoid any unnecessary misunderstandings.

Based on the previously mentioned viewpoint, bilingual ordinances in Hong Kong are classified as vocative texts. Therefore, the most important aspect of the translation process is to retain and convey the information and intention of the source text. A dynamic equivalence translation strategy should be then adopted. However, the translation of bilingual ordinances in Hong Kong is a special case due to its unique nature. As Hong Kong was a former British colony, the majority of legislation in Hong Kong was enacted during British rule. English was the sole official language, while Chinese was merely used for reference without legal effect.

However, prior to the handover of Hong Kong in 1997, it was required that certain important ordinances must be translated into Chinese and become Chinese legislation by going through legislative procedures. But Hong Kong translators are still under the great influence of English thinking patterns, so the Chinese translations they produced cannot quickly get rid of the constraints of English. This has led to the adoption of the translation strategy of 'literal translation' rather than 'dynamic equivalence' for Chinese translations of Hong Kong legislation. For example, after the promulgation of Chinese legislation in Hong Kong, there were widespread criticisms. Such criticism was reported in the *Ming Pao* newspaper on 12 May 1997 (cited in Wang, 2006: 59–60):

> Starting from the middle of this month, all Hong Kong ordinances will have their Chinese versions. However, legal professionals have pointed out that the Chinese versions are often not fluent and are difficult to understand. The lawyer Barbara Hung, who specialises in family law, attended a seminar on 'Choosing to Remarry' organised by the Christian Family Service Centre yesterday. She stated that Hong Kong legislation is now officially bilingual, theoretically having Chinese translations for all legislation. However, many lawyers primarily study English, so they have a limited understanding of the Chinese versions of the legislation. In general, they refer to the English versions when dealing with legal matters and only consult the Chinese translations when necessary. Barbara Hung pointed out that there are many areas in the Chinese translations that are not smooth, making it difficult even for those who understand Chinese. She mentioned that many translated provisions leave them puzzled because they rely on their knowledge of English to make sense of the Chinese translations. However, if reading the Chinese versions alone, they find it a challenging task.

This is true. General readers find both Chinese and English legal texts difficult to understand. However, from the discussion of legal professionals in the context of Hong Kong's bilingual legal system, it becomes apparent that the Chinese translations are even more challenging to comprehend than the original English texts. This is primarily because an overly literal translation strategy is adopted in the translation process. In other words, complete dynamic equivalence is not realised in Hong Kong's legal translation, as applying dynamic equivalence would require using legal concepts from the legal system in the target language for the translation of legal concepts. This would jeopardise the preservation of the original intention and function of the legal concepts expressed in the source text. Therefore, in the process of translating texts involving two legal systems (including Hong Kong), translators must keep and follow the legal concepts of the legal system in the source text when translating legal concepts. It is unnecessary to consider whether the readers of the translated texts are familiar with these 'unfamiliar' legal concepts. In spite of this, nowadays, Chinese translation in Hong Kong is no longer overly literal or too rigid, thanks to the vigorous promotion of Chinese by the Hong Kong government. And the Chinese language has increasingly gained more influence in Hong Kong.

According to Šarčević (1997: 24), the development of legal translation can be illustrated on the continuum: strict literal → literal → moderately literal → near idiomatic → idiomatic → co-drafting. It can be seen that translators have progressively gained more freedom, going through phrases from strict literal translation to co-drafting. Co-drafting represents the final phase of development, as seen in some bilingual or multilingual regions like Canada that have implemented bilingual drafting. Bilingual drafting is not only a product of legal translation at a certain phase of development, but also a viable translation strategy. For example, Hong Kong's Basic Law is a successful example of bilingual drafting. This principle applies similarly to translations involving two different legal systems. Therefore, to faithfully convey the intention consistent with the source text, bilingual drafting is the optimal translation strategy, ensuring consistency with the original intention. However, currently, the translation of the majority of laws and ordinances in Hong Kong is not done by co-drafting. This is because Hong Kong does not yet possess the essential conditions for co-drafting. Factors such as the bilingual proficiency of legislators, resources, and other constraints limit this possibility. For instance, legislators and translators may not be able to be present simultaneously, and the availability of qualified translators is another challenge. Therefore, co-drafting can only be seen as a future trend in legal translation.

3.4 Summary

This chapter, by reviewing and summarising text typology, highlights the limitations of previous scholars' perspectives on legal text types. Subsequently, a new perspective on legal text types is put forward, i.e., the function of legal texts is vocative when the function of translated texts is consistent with that of the source text. However, when the function of translated texts differs, the function of the source text is vocative and the function of the translated texts can be either informative or expressive. Based on this premise, translation strategies for legal texts are further discussed: a 'word-for-word' translation strategy is still employed for the translation of Hong Kong legislative provisions due to the special context of Hong Kong.

In the following chapter, this book focuses on discussing the translation of conditional clauses in the Companies Ordinance. As both versions of the Hong Kong bilingual legislation are equally authentic, the function of the translated texts being consistent with that of the source text, the bilingual texts of Hong Kong legislation can be considered vocative texts. Based on this foundation, a detailed analysis of various translations of introductory words for conditional clauses in the Companies Ordinance is conducted, with a view to examining whether these different translations achieve the same function as the original text.

References

Baker, Mona. (ed.). *Routledge Encyclopaedia of Translation Studies*. London; New York: Routledge, 1998.

Bühler, Karl. *Theory of Language: The Representational Function of Language* (Trans. Donald Fraser Goodwin, 1990). Amsterdam; Philadelphia: John Benjamins Publishing Company, 1965.

Delisle, Jean. *Translation: An Interpretative Approach*. Ottawa: University of Ottawa Press, 1988.

House, Juliane. *Translation Quality Assessment: A Model Revisited*. Tübingen: Gunter Narr Verlag, 1997.

Newmark, Peter. *Approaches to Translation*. Oxford: Pergamon, 1982.

Newmark, Peter. *A Textbook of Translation*. New York: Prentice-Hall International, 1988.

Nida, Eugene. *Toward A Science of Translating: With Special Reference to Principles and Procedures Involved in Bible Translating*. Leiden: E.J. Brill, 1964.

Nord, Christiane. *Translating as A Purposeful Activity: Functionalist Approaches Explained.* Manchester: St. Jerome Publishing, 1997.
Reiss, Christina. *Translation Criticism: Potential and Limitations* (Trans. Erroll F. Rhodes). Manchester: St. Jerome Publishing, 1971.
Robinson, Douglas. *Western Translation Theory: From Herodotus to Nietzsche*. Manchester: St. Jerome Publishing, 1997.
Sager, Juan C. *Language Engineering and Translation: Consequences of Automation.* Amsterdam; Philadelphia: John Benjamins Publishing Company, 1993.
Šarčević, Susan. *New Approach to Legal Translation.* The Hague; Boston: Kluwer Law International, 1997.
Snell-Hornby, Mary. *Translation Studies: An Integrated Approach.* Amsterdam; Philadelphia: John Benjamins Publishing Company, 1988.

Jiang, Jianyun [姜劍雲]. 法律語言與言語研究 [*Legal Language and Discourse Research*]. 北京：群眾出版社 [Beiing: Qunzhong Publishing House], 1995.
Li, Kexing [李克興]. 論法律文本的靜態對等翻譯 [On static equivalence in translating legal texts]. 外語教學與研究 [*Foreign Language Teaching and Research*], 2010 (1): 59–61.
Teng, Chao & Kong, Feiyan [騰超、孔飛燕]. 英漢法律互譯：理論與實踐 [*English-Chinese Legal Translation: Theory & Practice*]. 杭州：浙江大學出版社 [Hangzhou: Zhejiang University Press], 2008.
Wang, Daogeng [王道庚]. 法律翻譯：理論與實踐 [*Legal Translation – Theory and Practice*]. 香港：香港城市大學出版社 [Hong Kong: City University of Hong Kong Press], 2006.

4 Translation of conditional clauses in Hong Kong bilingual ordinances

4.1 Introductory words for conditional clauses

4.1.1 Introduction of introductory words for conditional clauses

As a special text type, a legal text has its own textual features in various aspects such as diction, syntax, and style. One of the syntactic features is the complexity of sentence structures in long legal sentences, with such common modifiers as attributive clauses, adverbial clauses, nominal clauses, adjectival clauses, past participles, present participles, and appositive phrases, amongst others. Some single legal articles can be as long as one paragraph, which is actually only one sentence. According to Barber (1962), the average length of legal sentences is 271 words, compared with an average length of only 27.6 words for sentences used in science and technology English texts. Bhatia (1993: 110), when discussing syntax features of legal articles, observes that 'the legal subject is conventionally delayed by the introduction of a long case description in the form of an adverbial clause beginning with "where", "if" or sometimes "when".' Frequent use of adverbial clauses is an important feature of legal texts, and therefore understanding the usage and translation of conditional clauses would greatly enhance the translation efficiency of legal texts. In this chapter, various conditional clauses and their translation patterns are discussed in detail.

Based on the statistics generalised in this study, in the Companies Ordinance of Hong Kong Bilingual Ordinances, there are a total of 2,247 full sentences (calculated by the use of a full stop), 987 of which include at least 1 introductory word of conditional clauses, making up about 44%. The data and percentage demonstrate the importance of conditional clauses in the Companies Ordinance and foreground syntactic features of legal texts.

Li (2008) introduces common introductory words of conditional clauses and their translations; eight main introductory words ('if,' 'where,' 'when,' 'in case,' 'in the event,' 'should,' 'provided,' and 'providing') are discussed in terms of their usage and differences. Based on those common introductory words, a starting point and useful reference for this book, this book attempts to check and explore the specific usage and translation of such introductory words in the sample text, i.e., the Companies Ordinance.

DOI: 10.4324/9781003359180-4

4.1.2 Introductory words for conditional clauses in the Companies Ordinance

In the whole Companies Ordinance, there are five introductory words for conditional clauses: 'if,' 'where,' 'when,' 'in the event,' and 'in (the) case.' The frequency and percentage of each introductory word are shown in Table 4.1.

Table 4.1 Frequency and percentage of introductory words for conditional clauses in the Companies Ordinance

Introductory words for conditional clauses	*Frequency*	*Percentage*
If	872	45
Where	668	34
When	73	4
In (the) case	289	15
In the event	37	2

From Table 4.1, not all bilingual ordinances include all of the eight introductory words of conditional clauses mentioned in Section 4.1.1, and not all such introductory words are used to introduce conditional clauses. To be more specific,

(1) 'Provided that' occurs 110 times in the Companies Ordinance, but it is used in the form of 'proviso.' According to *Modern Chinese Dictionary* (2005: 268), 'proviso' refers to the part followed by '但'(dàn; but) or '但是' (dàn shì; but) in legal provisions, meaning the exception or limitation of such provisions. There is no sign of 'providing that' in the same text.
(2) 'Should' occurs in the Companies Ordinance as its original meaning of '應該' (yīng gāi; ought to) or '應當' (yīng dāng; ought to), instead of introducing conditional clauses.
(3) 'In the event' occurs only 37 times, which are respectively translated as '如' (rú; if) 20 times, and '一旦' (yī dàn; in case) 8 times, '在 …… 時' (zài …… shí; when) 7 times, '凡' (fán; where) once, and '在 …… 情況下' (zài …… qíng kuàng xià; under the circumstance of) once.
(4) 'When' occurs 73 times in the text, serving most of the time as an introductory word for the adverbial clause for time, except that it is translated 5 times as '如' (rú; if).
(5) 'In (the) case' occurs 273 times, and 'in case' occurs 16 times, most of which is translated as '如' (rú; if).
(6) A good majority of introductory words of conditional clauses are 'if' and 'where,' which occur 875 times and 668 times separately, each making up 45% and 34%.

4.1.3 Comparing introductory words in English conditional clauses

This section analyses and compares similarities and differences between the meaning and usage of a few introductory words of conditional clauses. 'If' is the most common one with a variety of usage. According to *English-Chinese Dictionary* (Lu, 2007: 871), 'if' has the following entries:

(1a) as conjunction for expressing conditions or hypotheses: '假如' (jiǎ rú), '如果' (rú guǒ), '要是' (yào shi); 即使(jí shǐ), 縱令 (zòng lìng), 雖然 (suī rán); 無論何時 (wú lùn hé shí), 當 (dāng); 是否 (shì fǒu);
(1b) as conjunction for expressing wishes, followed by concluding sentences without conditional clauses: 要是 ...... 多好 (yào shi ...... duō hǎo);
(1c) as conjunction for expressing surprise, depression or anger, used together with the negative form of verbs;
(1d) as conjunction for expressing a polite request, used together with 'will', 'can' or 'would' etc.;
(2a) as noun for expressing conditions, regulations or hypotheses;
(2b) as noun for expressing doubts or doubtful issues.

'If' in daily life or in other texts is used with diversified translations, basically near-synonyms of '如' (rú), '如果' (rú guǒ), '假如' (jiǎ rú), '假若' (jiǎ ruò), '要是' (yào shi), or '倘若' (tǎng ruò). But 'if' in legal texts is generally used as a conjunction for expressing conditions or hypotheses, and its translation is primarily '如' (rú).

From *English-Chinese Dictionary* (Lu, 2007: 2167), 'where' can be used as an adverb, conjunction, pronoun, or noun, with the common meaning of '在哪裡' (zài nǎ lǐ) or '在 ...... 地方' (zài ...... dì fāng). But in the legal context, 'where' (especially when it appears at the beginning of a sentence) is regarded as an introductory word for conditional clauses. Or more precisely, it is used to introduce a certain case or circumstance, in spite of the fact that a good number of the instances of 'where' are translated as '如' (rú), the same as the translation of 'if.'

'If' and 'where' are the two most frequently used introductory words in the Companies Ordinance, so what is the difference between those two words in terms of usage and translation?

In respect of 'if' and 'where,' Coode (1848) believes that there lies a significant difference, i.e., 'if' expresses conditions of enforcing an obligation or another, while 'where' expresses certain circumstances or occasions. But his theory was proposed in the 19th century. Does such a difference still exist in the modern text of the Companies Ordinance? This book attempts to explore their differences from a number of sentences including both 'if' and 'where.'

Example 1: **Where** a company refuses to register any person as a member in respect of shares which have been transmitted to him by operation of law, that person shall be entitled to call on the company to furnish a statement of the reasons for the refusal, and, **if** the company fails to furnish such statement within a period of 28 days after the request therefor, the company shall, on the expiration of that period, register the transfer forthwith.

Chinese translation: 凡公司拒絕就某人已藉法律的施行而獲傳轉的股份，登記該人為成員，該人有權請求公司提供一份拒絕理由陳述書，如公司在該項請求提出後28天內未有提供該份陳述書，則公司須在有關期限屆滿時，立即登記該宗轉讓。

In this example, 'where' is translated as '凡' (fán; where) and 'if' as '如' (rú; if). As seen from the conditional clause introduced by 'where,' such a case that 'a company refuses to register any person as a member in respect of shares which have been transmitted to him by operation of law' is introduced. And the 'where' clause can be replaced by a more common expression, i.e., 'any … who …' So here we can also say: 'Any company which refuses to register any person as a member in respect of shares which have been transmitted to him by operation of law,' in which the defining attributive clause is used to express a condition. Such an expression 'any … who …' is common in the Companies Ordinance. For instance, 'Any person who publishes or discloses any information or document in contravention of subsection (1) shall be guilty of an offence and liable to imprisonment and a fine.' The Chinese translation is '任何人如違反第(1)款而發表或披露任何資料或文件，即屬犯罪，可處監禁及罰款。' 'Any person who …' is translated as '任何人如' (rèn hé rén rú), equal to '凡' (fán), whose meaning indicates 'all, everything, anything,' etc. By contrast, '如' (rú) introduces a pure condition that 'the company fails to furnish such statement within a period of 28 days after the request therefor.' In such a case and under such a condition, the main clause introduces the actual action taken by the company: 'the company shall, on the expiration of that period, register the transfer forthwith.'

Example 2: **<u>Where</u>** a limited company is plaintiff in any action or other legal proceeding, any judge having jurisdiction in the matter may, **<u>if</u>** it appears by credible testimony that there is reason to believe that the company will be unable to pay the costs of the defendant if successful in his defence, require sufficient security to be given for those costs, and may stay all proceedings until the security is given.

Chinese translation: 凡一間有限公司在任何訴訟或其他法律程序中為原告人，任何在有關事宜上具有司法管轄權的法官，如依據可信證供而覺得有理由相信在被告人勝訴時，該公司將無力支付被告人的訟費，則該法官可規定該公司須就該等訟費給予一充分保證，並可擱置所有法律程序，直至該公司給予該項保證為止。

In this example, 'where' refers to such a case that 'a limited company is plaintiff in any action or other legal proceeding,' i.e., the legal subject is not included in such a case. Therefore, 'where' is translated as '凡' (fán). And 'if' is used to introduce a hypothetical condition, i.e., 'it appears by credible testimony that there is reason to believe that the company will be unable to pay the costs of the defendant if successful in his defence.' Compared with the 'where' clause, the 'if' clause introduces a case of narrower scope, which is also a hypothetical condition based on the case stated in the previous 'where' clause. As such, the difference between 'where' and 'if' is clear in terms of sequence and focus as well as their translations.

> Example 3: **<u>Where</u>** the Official Receiver becomes the liquidator of a company, whether provisionally or otherwise, he may, **<u>if</u>** satisfied that the nature of the estate or business of the company, or the interests of the creditors or contributories generally, or there are other grounds therefor, require the appointment of a special manager of the estate or business of the company other than himself, apply to the court, and the court may on such application, appoint a special manager of the said estate or business to act during such time as the court may direct, with such powers, including any of the powers of a receiver or manager, as may be entrusted to him by the court.
>
> Chinese translation: 凡破產管理署署長成為公司的清盤人，不論是臨時或屬其他情況，如其信納基於公司的產業或業務性質，或基於債權人或分擔人的一般利益，或基於其他理由，需要在其本人以外另委一名公司產業或業務的特別經理人，則可向法院申請，而法院可應該申請而委任一名上述產業或業務的特別經理人，在法院所指示的期間內行事，該經理人並具有法院所托付的各項權力，其中包括接管人或經理人所具有的任何權力。

As in the previous two examples, 'where' in example 3 is also translated as '凡' (fán) and 'if' to '如' (rú). It can be seen that the situation introduced by ''where' seems to be more like a general case, covering a wider range of content, while 'if' simply introduces a condition, which is based on the situation introduced by 'where,' and the two words cannot be used interchangeably. In addition, the content introduced by 'where' is often more important than the content introduced by 'if,' and when the two appear in the same sentence, the content introduced by 'where' must occur before the conditional situation introduced by 'if.'

To sum up, the usage of conditional clauses introduced by 'if' is not much different from that in legal texts. However, the usage of conditional clauses introduced by 'where' is rarely seen in common texts or daily life, but its importance cannot be ignored in legal texts. Take the Companies Ordinance for example. Apart from the 872 conditional clauses introduced by 'if,' there are also as many as 668 conditional clauses introduced by 'where,' showing its important status in legal texts. In fact, 'where' used to be used to introduce conditional clauses long ago. There is an old proverb: 'Where there is a will, there is a way' (有志者事竟成; yǒu zhì zhě shì jìng chéng). Here 'where' is preferred to 'if' for two reasons: firstly, out of rhetorical considerations: 'where' rhymes with 'there'; secondly, 'if' does not carry the meaning of 'all, or everything.' Accordingly, the differences between 'if' and 'where' can be summarised below:

(1) Firstly, when 'where' is used to introduce a conditional clause, it carries the meaning of 'all, or everything,' and can be replaced with the sentence structure

of 'any … who …' But 'if' is just a word to introduce a simple conditional clause.

(2) Secondly, 'if' usually introduces a condition, while 'where' introduces a case or occasion.

However, many legal drafters and translators often mix up the two words, believing that they can be used interchangeably. Actually, there are still differences between them and they cannot be used in reverse order. Therefore, although modern laws are not as strict as ancient laws, the difference between 'if' and 'where' in conditional clauses can still be seen from the analysis of the conditional clauses introduced by them in the Hong Kong ordinances.

Another common introductory word 'when' includes two common meanings. Besides serving as an adverbial clause of time, 'when' can also be a conjunction introducing adverbial clauses of condition, similar to conditional clauses introduced by 'if.' For instance, 'When one Party removes and replaces any directors whom it has appointed, it shall give written notice to the other Parties, the former and newly appointed directors and the Joint Venture Company, and state the reasons therefor.' The Chinese translation is '如果一方要撤換任何董事，應向其他各方及原任董事、新任董事和合營公司發出書面通知，並說明撤換情由。' In this example, the condition clause of 'one Party removes and replaces any directors whom it has appointed' is introduced by 'when,' which can also be replaced by 'if,' without altering the meaning or structure of the original text.

With respect to 'in case' and 'in the event,' according to the online *Oxford English Dictionary*, 'in case' refers to 'in the event or contingency that; if it should prove or that; if,' while 'in case' is synonymous with 'in the event,' from which we can see that the meanings of these two phrases are very close. One interpretation of 'in the event' is 'undersigned or incidental result,' and 'in the event' means 'in the case (something specified) should occur,' expressing a hypothetical or assumed result, circumstance, or contingency, usually translated as '一旦' (yī dàn) or '萬一' (wàn yī).

Compared with 'if,' 'in the event' and 'in case' put more emphasis on contingency, that is, the chance of hypothetical conditions happening is small. Sometimes those two phrases are translated as '如果' (rú guǒ) or '假如' (jiǎ rú), but in contrast, 'if' is not translated as '一旦' (yī dàn) or '萬一' (wàn yī), from which we can see the difference between them.

4.1.4 Comparing introductory words in Chinese conditional clauses

'如果' (rú guǒ; if) is used to express hypothetical conditions in the Chinese conditional clauses, but in the text of the Companies Ordinance, similar Chinese expressions including '如' (rú), '假若' (jiǎ ruò), '假使' (jiǎ shǐ), '若' (ruò), '倘若' (tǎng ruò), and '一旦' (yī dàn) are used. So is there any difference among those expressions?

According to *Modern Chinese Word-Ocean Dictionary* (2002: 574), one of the explanations of '如' (rú) is '假使' (jiǎ shǐ) or '要是' (yào shi). But '如果' (rú guǒ) is interpreted as a hypothetical conjunction, with synonyms of '即使' (jí shǐ) or '倘若' (tǎng ruò). Besides, checking the entries of '假如' (jiǎ rú), '假使' (jiǎ shǐ), and '假若' (jiǎ ruò) leads to the interpretation of '如果' (rú guǒ) (2002: 318), and '若' (ruò) also to the interpretation of '假如' (jiǎ rú) or '如果' (rú guǒ) (2002: 578). '倘' (tǎng), '倘若' (tǎng ruò), and '倘使' (tǎng shǐ) are also conjunctions expressing hypotheses, meaning '假使' (jiǎ shǐ) or '如果' (rú guǒ) (2002: 659). Accordingly, all of the above terms '如' (rú), '如果' (rú guǒ), '倘若' (tǎng ruò), '假如' (jiǎ rú), '假使' (jiǎ shǐ), '假若' (jiǎ ruò), '倘' (tǎng), and '倘使' (tǎng shǐ) in the dictionary are conjunctions for hypotheses, without significant differences in meaning, and basically interchangeable.

However, Chao (1968), a Chinese linguist, thinks otherwise. These terms, differing in their expression of hypothetical possibilities, can be arranged in a continuum: 要是 (yào shi)/若是 (ruò shì) ➔ 要 (yào) ➔ 假如 (jiǎ rú) ➔ 若是 (ruò shì) ['如' (rú) and '若' (ruò) are confined to the archaic Chinese language (文言wén yán)] ➔ 倘若 (tǎng ruò) ➔ 假若 (jiǎ ruò) ➔ 假使 (jiǎ shǐ) ➔ 倘使 (tǎng shǐ) ➔ 设若 (shè ruò). The sequence shows the possibility from the highest to the lowest, and the likelihood from less likely to more likely to be used for hypotheses contrary to the fact.

However, Jiang (2000) believes that with the development of the modern Chinese language over the past few decades, some of these terms listed by Chao have been phased out, and those terms in current use also seem to be of little difference (barely noticeable by most native speakers) in the degree of hypotheses or counter-factuality. And '如果' (rú guǒ) and '假设' (jiǎ shè), commonly used in the modern Chinese language, should be added to Chao's list, and '如' (rú) and '若' (ruò) in Chao's list seem not to be confined to the archaic Chinese language.

Based on the above observations, we should take one step further to explore the usage in legal texts: is there any difference among these terms in the translation of legal provisions?

In addition to the above list, we also have the other two terms '一旦' (yī dàn) and '萬一' (wàn yī), similar to '如' (rú), whose difference in meanings can be differentiated. According to *Modern Chinese Word-Ocean Dictionary* (2002: 793), '一旦' (yī dàn) is a term expressing an uncertain time, referring to one day suddenly or hypothetically. From the interpretation, the possibility for things to happen is much lower than with '如' (rú). Similarly, '萬一' (wàn yī) expresses contingency of very low possibility or hypotheses of very small chances, generally interchangeable with '一旦' (yī dàn). '萬一' (wàn yī) is a conjunction derived from content words (shí cí). However, as a conjunction with subjunctive features, it can also be used with other hypothetical conjunctions such as '如果' (rú guǒ) or '要是' (yào shi) for the emphasis of the hypothetical tone. '萬一' (wàn yī), as a hypothetical conjunction, is used to express the speaker's belief that there is a very low possibility of happenings under normal circumstances, but without ruling out such a possibility, which arouses the speaker's thought or plan on the result or consequences if such a happening with low possibility indeed happens (Xu, 2002: 35). For example, 況且老婆和小寶也都得喝那水，萬一他們中的一個也得了那該死的病，先我而去我又怎麼辦呢？ [Literal translation: Not to mention both the wife and the kid have to drink the water, what if one of them got that damn disease and dies before me?] (Fang Fang's novel *Destiny* (定數; dìng shù). If '萬一' (wàn yī) in the sentence is replaced by '如果' (rú guǒ), then the contingency of 'getting the damn disease' emphasised in the original context will become less obvious.

In addition, '凡' (fán), a frequently used word in the Companies Ordinance, is inclusive of everything within a certain scope. So literally speaking, '凡' (fán) is more extensive and inclusive than '如' (rú), the latter emphasising the hypothetical occurrence of a certain happening. Therefore, the advantage of using '凡' (fán) lies in its brevity and conciseness, as it has the grammatical function of introducing conditional clauses, and also includes the meaning of 'everything.' With '凡' (fán) being used in a certain context, the language and style are more formal and professional, which is consistent with the formal style of legal texts, especially for such an authoritative and serious text of Hong Kong ordinances. However, there exists a difference between the diction of legal texts in Hong Kong and Mainland China: '凡' (fán) is used to introduce legal conditional clauses in Hong Kong, while '……的' (de) is used to express similar legal sentence structures in Mainland China.

4.2 Translation of different introductory words for conditional clauses

4.2.1 Conditional clauses introduced by 'if' and different translations of 'if'

In the Companies Ordinance, 'if' occurs 872 times, 776 of which are translated as '如' (rú). In this section, 'if' and its Chinese translation '如' (rú) are compared and examined.

'If' occurs 872 times in total in the Companies Ordinance, whose translations are listed in Table 4.2.

It can be seen that 'if' is dominantly translated as '如' (rú), accounting for 89%. 'If' can be understood to be equivalent to the Chinese expression '如' (rú). So under what circumstances 'if' is translated otherwise? Is there any special meaning for adopting other translations, or is it because of different translators' divergent choices? Do these translations achieve the same function as the original text? In

Table 4.2 Summary of different translations of 'if' in the Companies Ordinance

Translations of 'if'	*Frequency*		*Percentage*
如 (rú)	776		89
在 …… 時 (zài …… shí)	8	96	11
假若 (jiǎ ruò)	23		
若 (ruò)	7		
假使 (jiǎ shǐ)	3		
倘/倘若 (tǎng/tǎng ruò)	3		
不譯 (no translation)	26		
在 …… 情況下 (zài …… qíngkuàng xià)	26		

this section, such translation methods, except for '如' (rú), are selected for detailed analysis.

(I) 'If' translated as '假若' (jiǎ ruò)

There are in total 22 sentences in which 'if' is translated as '假若' (jiǎ ruò), as shown in Table 4.3.

From these 'if' conditional clauses, except for sentence No. 6 which uses the present tense or present perfect tense, all of the rest of the 21 sentences use the subjunctive mood, such as 'were,' 'had continued,' or 'had been enacted.'

In sentence No. 1, an 'if' conditional clause is already used before the clause 'if it were a society in respect of which the Societies Ordinance applied,' in which 'if' is translated as '如' (rú), so when 'if' occurs for the second time, it is translated as '假若' (jiǎ ruò) to avoid repetition. But the most important reason is that the second occurrence of 'if' is used to introduce the subjunctive mood, which means that what the speaker says is not a fact, but a hypothesis, wish, suspicion, or guess. The subjunctive mood used in non-factual conditional clauses expresses hypothetical or unlikely circumstances, which can be contrary to the present fact, the past fact, or even the future fact. It is worth noting that only non-factual conditional clauses use the subjunctive mood. From the meaning of the sentence, we can know whether the hypothetical condition can be realised. If yes, then the subjunctive mood cannot be used; if no, then the subjunctive mood should be used. As we know, such terms as '如' (rú), '假若' (jiǎ ruò), and '假如' (jiǎ rú) are introductory words for hypothetical conditions, and they are also deemed to be synonyms or near-synonyms of '如' (rú) in Chinese dictionaries and daily life. However, when the subjunctive mood is used in non-factual conditional clauses in legal provisions, the Chinese translation is '假若' (jiǎ ruò), which means that the wording difference between '如' (rú) and '假若' (jiǎ ruò) is noticed by legal translators—the latter indicating very low likelihood or unlikelihood.

Take sentence No. 15 as another example: 'the resolution would not have been passed **if** he had not done so.' The subjunctive mood is used to indicate that such members had already made such a resolution, and would be unlikely to change it in the future. And such a resolution had been passed, which is a hypothetical case contrary to the fact. Therefore, the translation is '**假若**該等成員不曾如此表決，則該項決議不會獲通過。'

Sentence No. 19 also uses the subjunctive mood, in which 'if living' is the abbreviated form of 'if he were living,' which means that a deceased member of a company would have had the same rights if he were living. However, it is obviously impossible for the deceased member to come back to life, so this is also a hypothetical case that would not happen. Therefore the translation is '公司已故成員的合法遺產代理人，在各方面均須視為該公司的成員，具有有關出席公司會議並表決的權利，與已故成員**假若**在生本會具有的權利相同。'

Based on the specific analysis of the above few examples, we can tell the subtle difference between '如' (rú) and '假若' (jiǎ ruò) in legal provisions. That is, when

Table 4.3 'If' translated as '假若' (jiă ruò)

No.	*English original*	*Chinese translation*
1	If the Chief Executive in Council is satisfied that a company to which Part XI applies would, **<u>if</u>** it were a society in respect of which the Societies Ordinance (Cap 151) applied, be liable to have- (a) …; or (b) …,	如行政長官會同行政會議信納，第XI部所適用的公司**假若**是《社團條例》(第151章)所適用的社團— (a) ……；或 (b) ……，
2	In the event of the accounts being audited by a public servant there shall be paid to the Government in respect of such audit a sum equal to the fee which would have been chargeable on the audit of the Official Receiver's accounts **<u>if</u>** the winding up had been a winding up by the court.	如帳目由一名公務員審計，則須就上述審計向政府支付一筆款項，數額等於清盤**假若**是一宗由法院作出的清盤本會就審計破產管理署署長的帳目所征收的費用。
3	Next, in paying to the Government a sum equal to the fees which the Official Receiver could lawfully have charged **<u>if</u>** he had acted as liquidator of the company in a winding up thereof by the court.	再其次，向政府繳付一筆款項，數額相等於破產管理署署長**假若**在法院將該公司清盤時曾充當該公司清盤人本可合法地收取的費用。
4	Where any person to whom this section applies has reason to apprehend that any claim will or might be made against him in respect of any negligence, default, breach of duty or breach of trust, he may apply to the court for relief, and the court on any such application shall have the same power to relieve him as under this section it would have had **<u>if</u>** it had been a court before which proceedings against that person for negligence, default, breach of duty or breach of trust had been brought.	凡本條適用的人有理由憂慮會有或可能有任何有關疏忽、失責、失職或違反信托行為的申索向其提出，該人可向法院申請給予寬免，而法院在接獲任何此等申請時，有權根據本條寬免該人，猶如針對該人的疏忽、失責、失職或違反信托行為的法律程序**假若**在該法院席前提出則該法院本會有該項權力一樣。
5	Where any document by which any shares in or debentures of a company incorporated outside Hong Kong are offered for sale to the public would, **<u>if</u>** the company concerned had been a company within the meaning of this Ordinance, have been deemed by virtue of section 41 to be a prospectus issued by the company, that document shall be deemed to be, for the purposes of this Part of this Ordinance, a prospectus issued by the company.	凡就在香港以外成立為法團的公司的股份或債權證向公眾作出要約發售， **假若**有關公司是本條例所指的公司則該要約所據的文件本會憑借第41條 當作是招股章程者，為施行本條例本部的規定， 該份文件須當作是該公司 所發出的招股章程。

(*Continued*)

Table 4.3 (Continued)

No.	*English original*	*Chinese translation*
6	Where any non-Hong Kong company makes default in delivering to the Registrar the name and address of a person resident in Hong Kong authorized to accept on behalf of the company service of process or notices, or **if** at any time all the persons whose names and addresses have been so delivered are dead or have ceased so to reside or refuse to accept service on behalf of the company or for any reason cannot be served, a document may be served on the company-	凡任何非香港公司沒有將居於香港並獲授權代表公司接受送達法律程序文件或通知書的人的姓名及地址交付處長，或**假若**所有姓名及地址已如此交付的人均已去世，或已不再居於香港，或拒絕代表公司接受送達法律程序文件或通知書，或因任何原因不能送達文件，則文件可以下述方式送達該公司—
7	Subject to subsection (1A), in the case of a company which has been dissolved under section 226A, 227, 239 or 248, the court may at any time within 2 years of the date of the dissolution, on an application being made for the purpose by the liquidator of the company or by any other person who appears to the court to be interested, make an order, upon such terms as the court thinks fit, declaring the dissolution to have been void, and thereupon such proceedings may be taken as might have been taken **if** the company had not been dissolved.	除第(1A)款另有規定外，如公司已根據第226A、227、239或248條解散，法院可在解散日期起計2年內的任何時間，應公司的清盤人或法院覺得有利害關係的任何其他人為有關目的而提出的申請，按法院認為合適的條款作出命令，宣布解散無效，而**假若**公司未曾解散則可能已予進行的法律程序即可隨即進行。
8	Section 5(a) of the Protection of Wages on Insolvency (Amendment) Ordinance 1996 (68 of 1996) ('the amending Ordinance') shall not apply in the case of a winding up to which an application under section 15(1) of the Protection of Wages on Insolvency Ordinance (Cap 380) relates where such application is made before the commencement of the amending Ordinance, and in such a case, the provisions relating to preferential payments which would have applied **if** the amending Ordinance had not been enacted shall be deemed to remain in full force.	在任何與根據《破產欠薪保障條例》(第380章)第15(1)條作出的申請有關的清盤中，如提出該申請的日期是在《1996年破產欠薪保障(修訂)條例》(1996年第68號)("修訂條例")生效之前，則在該宗清盤中，修訂條例第5(a)條不適用，而在該情況下，**假若**修訂條例不曾制定則會適用的關於優先付款的條文，須當作仍然完全有效。

9	The Companies (Amendment) (No. 3) Ordinance 1988 (79 of 1988) shall not apply in the case of a winding up where the date of the commencement of the winding up occurred before the commencement of that Ordinance, and, in such a case, the provisions relating to preferential payments which would have applied <u>**if**</u> that Ordinance had not been enacted shall be deemed to remain in full force.	凡在任何清盤中，清盤開始日期是在《1988年公司(修訂)(第3號)條例》#(1988年第79號)生效之前，則該條例不適用於該宗清盤，而在該情況下，**假若**該條例未曾制定本會適用的關於優先付款的條文，須當作仍然完全有效。
10	The Fourth Schedule to the Protection of Wages on Insolvency Ordinance 1985 (12 of 1985) shall not apply in the case of a winding up where the date of the commencement of the winding up occurred before the commencement+ of that Ordinance, and, in such case, the provisions relating to preferential payments which would have applied <u>**if**</u> that Ordinance had not been enacted shall be deemed to remain in full force.	凡在任何清盤中，清盤開始日期是在《1985年破產欠薪保障條例》++(1985年第12號)生效+之前，則該條例的附表4不適用於該宗清盤，而在該情況下，**假若**該條例未曾制定本會適用的關於優先付款的條文，須當作仍然完全有效。
11	The Companies (Amendment) Ordinance 1984 (6 of 1984) shall not apply in the case of a winding up where the relevant date occurred before the commencement of that Ordinance, and, in such a case, the provisions relating to preferential payments which would have applied <u>**if**</u> that Ordinance had not been enacted shall be deemed to remain in full force.	凡在任何清盤中，有關日期是在《1984年公司(修訂)條例》@(1984年第6號)生效之前，則該條例不適用於該宗清盤，而在該情況下，**假若**該條例未曾制定則會適用的關於優先付款的條文，須當作仍然完全有效。
12	The liquidator or any contributory or creditor may apply to the court to determine any question arising in the winding up of a company, or to exercise, as respects the enforcing of calls, or any other matter, all or any of the powers which the court might exercise <u>**if**</u> the company were being wound up by the court.	清盤人或任何分擔人或債權人可向法院申請，要求就公司清盤過程中所產生的任何問題作出裁定，或就強制執行催繳或任何其他事宜，行使公司**假若**由法院清盤則法院可行使的所有或任何權力。
13	Where a contract is ratified by virtue of this section, the person who purported to act for or on behalf of the company in making the contract shall not thereafter be under any greater liability than he would have been <u>**if**</u> he had entered into the contract on behalf of the company as an agent acting without its authority and after its incorporation.	凡任何合約憑借本條而獲追認，則在訂立合約時其意是代表該公司行事的人，在該合約獲得追認後所須承擔的法律責任，不得大於**假若**該人是在該公司成立後未獲該公司授權而以代理人身分代表公司訂立合約的情況下所須承擔者。

(Continued)

Table 4.3 (Continued)

No.	*English original*	*Chinese translation*
14	In a case where the financial assistance is or includes a non-cash asset, any profit which, **if** the company were to make a distribution of that asset, would under section 79L be available for that purpose	如該項資助是一項非現金資產或包括一項非現金資產，則包括**假若**該公司分發該項資產時即會根據第79L條成為可供分發的任何利潤
15	A special resolution to confer, vary, revoke or renew authority under subsection (3) is not effective if any member of the company holding shares to which the resolution relates exercises the voting rights carried by any of those shares in voting on the resolution and the resolution would not have been passed **if** he had not done so.	根據第(3)款授予、更改、撤銷或重訂權限的特別決議，在下述情況中並無效力：持有與該項決議有關的股份的公司成員，行使該等股份所附有的表決權，就該項決議進行表決，而**假若**該等成員不曾如此表決，則該項決議不會獲通過。
16	The resolution is ineffective if any member of the company holding shares to which the resolution relates exercises the voting rights carried by any of those shares in voting on the resolution and the resolution would not have been passed **if** he had not done so.	該項決議在下述情況中並無效力：持有與該項決議有關的股份的公司成員，行使該等股份所附有的表決權，就該項決議進行表決，而**假若**該等成員不曾如此表決，則該項決議不會獲通過。
17	A person authorized under subsection (1) shall be entitled to exercise the same powers on behalf of the corporation which he represents as that corporation could exercise **if** it were an individual shareholder, creditor, or holder of debentures, of the company.	任何根據第(1)款獲授權的人，有權代其所代表的法團行使權力，該等權力與該法團**假若**是公司的個人股東、債權人或債權證持有人時所能行使的權力相同。
18	A person authorized under subsection (1A) shall be entitled to exercise the same powers on behalf of the recognized clearing house (or its nominee) which he represents as that clearing house (or its nominee) could exercise **if** it were an individual shareholder of the company.	任何根據第(1A)款獲授權的人，有權代其所代表的認可結算所(或其代名人)行使權力，該等權力與該結算所(或其代名人)**假若**是公司的個人股東時所能行使的權力相同。
19	The legal personal representative of a deceased member of a company shall, for the purposes of this section, be treated in all respects as a member of the company having the same rights with respect to attending and voting at a meeting of the company as such deceased member would, **if** living, have had.	就本條而言，公司已故成員的合法遺產代理人，在各方面均須視為該公司的成員，具有有關出席公司會議並表決的權利，與已故成員**假若**在生本會具有的權利相同。

20	Where any debentures which have been redeemed before the commencement of this Ordinance are re-issued subsequently to that date, the re-issue of the debentures shall not prejudice and shall be deemed never to have prejudiced any right or priority which any person would have had under or by virtue of any mortgage or charge created before the commencement of this Ordinance, **if** section 106 of the Companies Ordinance 1911 (58 of 1911), as originally enacted, had been enacted in this Ordinance instead of this section.	凡任何債權證在本條例生效前已贖回，並且在該生效日期後重新發行，則該等債權證的重新發行，對於**假若**原來制定的《1911年公司條例》(1911年第58號)第106條而非本條已在本條例中制定的話，任何人則會根據或憑借本條例生效前所設定的按揭或押記而享有的任何權利或優先權並無損害，而且當作從來對該等權利或優先權並無損害。
21	Where the shares or stock of a company have by amalgamation or otherwise become the shares or stock of another company, that other company shall have the same power under this section as the original company would have had **if** it had continued.	凡公司的股份或股額已因合並或其他原因成為另一間公司的股份或股額，則該另一間公司同樣具有本條所訂的權力，與原本的公司**假若**繼續營業時會具有的權力相同。
22	An auditor of a company would be so disqualified **if** the undertaking were a company	**假若**該企業是一間公司則會喪失獲委任為其核數師資格的人。

the subjunctive mood is used in non-factual conditional sentences in English, the corresponding translation in Chinese is ‘假若’ (jiǎ ruò) rather than ‘如’ (rú).

Therefore, when a non-factual conditional sentence introduced by ‘if’ uses the subjunctive mood, it expresses a hypothetical situation that may be contrary to the past, present, or future facts, indicating that such a situation has occurred and is unlikely to change or is less likely to occur in the future. But in general legal texts such as contracts, conditional sentences are generally introduced by ‘should,’ indicating a stronger hypothetical tone and translated as ‘萬一’ (wàn yī). For example,

> Should either of the parties to the contract be prevented from executing the contract by force majeure, such as earthquake, typhoon, flood, fire, war, etc., the prevented party shall notify the other party by cable without any delay, and within 15 days thereafter provide the detailed information of the events.

The Chinese translation is ‘合同任何一方，假如遇地震、台風、水災、火災、戰爭等不可抗力情況而不能履行合同時，應立即將該情況電報通知對方，並在事發後的15天內提供詳情。’ This sentence is selected from a sales contract, expressing less frequent force majeure (e.g., natural disasters). So the subjunctive conditional sentence introduced by ‘should’ is used to indicate the low probability of occurrence.

(II) ‘If’ translated as ‘假使’ (jiǎ shǐ)

There are three sentences in which ‘if’ is translated as ‘假使’ (jiǎ shǐ), as shown in Table 4.4.

In these examples, a non-factual conditional sentence introduced by ‘if’ uses the subjunctive mood to express a hypothetical situation or a situation contrary to facts, i.e., ‘had been created,’ ‘had been leased or hired,’ and ‘had been entered into.’ This is similar to the first translation where ‘if’ is translated as ‘假若’ (jiǎ ruò). During the translation process, the translator noticed a difference in tone between ‘假若’ (jiǎ ruò) and ‘假使’ (jiǎ shǐ), the latter expressing a higher degree of hypothesis. Take sentence No. 2 as an example: ‘if the goods had been leased or hired or the land had been leased on the open market, to a person who is unconnected with the company.’ The subjunctive mood is used to indicate a hypothetical situation of ‘the goods being leased or hired or the land being leased on the open market to a person unconnected with the company,’ which is contrary to the facts or has a very low likelihood of occurrence in the future.

(III) ‘If’ translated as ‘若’ (ruò)

There are seven sentences in which ‘if’ is translated as ‘若’ (ruò), as shown in Table 4.5.

In non-factual conditional sentences No. 3, 4, 5, and 6, the subjunctive mood is used with expressions such as ‘had been formed,’ ‘(it were) not for,’ ‘(it were)

Table 4.4 'If' translated as '假使' (jiǎ shǐ)

No.	*English original*	*Chinese translation*
1	**<u>If</u>** it had been created by the company or the property had been acquired after the company has been so registered, have been required to be registered under this Part, the company shall, within 5 weeks after it is so registered, deliver to the Registrar for registration the particulars in the specified form (including any instrument or its copy by which the charge was created or is evidenced) that are mentioned in this Part as requiring registration in respect of a charge of that kind.	該押記所屬類別為**假使**該押記是在該公司如此註冊後才由該公司設定(或**假使**該公司是在如此註冊後才獲取該財產)即鬚根據本部登記者，則該公司須在它如此註冊後的5個星期內，將本部所提及須就該類別押記而登記的詳情(包括該押記藉以設定或獲證明的任何文書或其副本)，以指明格式交付處長登記。
2	Leasing or hiring goods or leasing land to a director of the company on terms not more favourable than the terms it is reasonable to expect the company to have offered, **<u>if</u>** the goods had been leased or hired or the land had been leased on the open market, to a person who is unconnected with the company.	將貨物出租或租賃予或將土地出租予該公司的董事，而出租或租賃的條款與**假使**在公開市場將該貨物出租或租賃予或將該土地出租予與該公司沒有關連的人時可合理預期該公司會提供的條款相比，並不較為優惠。
3	Another person enters into a transaction or arrangement that, **<u>if</u>** it had been entered into by the company, would have contravened subsection (2), (3), (4) or (5).	某公司以外的另一人訂立**假使**由該公司訂立即會屬違反第(2)、(3)、(4)或(5)款的交易或安排。

created,' and 'had been created.' This is similar to the first two translations when 'if' is translated as '假若' (jiǎ ruò) or '假使' (jiǎ shǐ), indicating a hypothetical situation that is contrary to facts, that has already happened in the past and is unlikely to change, or that has a small likelihood of occurrence in the future. In the other three sentences No. 1, 2, and 7, 'if' introduces a factual conditional sentence, and '若' (ruò) and '如' (rú) can be considered synonymous and interchangeable because both have the same meaning and function as the original text. For example, '則**若**於載有該項押記的契據簽立後5個星期內' in sentence No. 7 can also be translated as '則**如**於載有該項押記的契據簽立後5個星期內.'

(IV)**'If' translated as '倘' (tǎng) or '倘若' (tǎng ruò)**

There are three sentences in which 'if' is translated as '倘' (tǎng) or '倘若' (tǎng ruò), as shown in Table 4.6.

In these three sentences, 'if' introduces a factual conditional sentence, and '倘' (tǎng) and '倘若' (tǎng ruò) can be considered synonymous and interchangeable with '如' (rú) because they have the same meaning and function as the original text. For example, in the first sentence, '**倘**在招股章程發出後38天內，仍有任何該等款項未如此退還' can also be translated as '**如**在招股章程發出後38天內，仍有任何該等款項未如此退還.'

Table 4.5 'If' translated as '若' (ruò)

No.	*English original*	*Chinese translation*
1	It does not include any payment in respect of 2 or more persons **if** the amount paid in respect of each of them is not ascertainable.	若就2人或多於2人支付款項，而就每個人所支付的款額不能確定者，則供款並不包括該等款項在內。
2	**If** the applicant is a company, it must nominate a person to be given notice of the deregistration.	申請人若是一間公司，則必須提名一人負責接收撤銷註冊通知書。
3	All provisions contained in any Ordinance or other instrument constituting or regulating the company, including, in the case of a company registered as a company limited by guarantee, the resolution declaring the amount of the guarantee, shall be deemed to be conditions and regulations of the company, in the same manner and with the same incidents as if so much thereof as would, **if** the company had been formed under this Ordinance, have been required to be inserted in the memorandum, were contained in a registered memorandum, and the residue thereof were contained in registered articles.	所有載於任何組織或規管該公司的條例或其他文書的條文，包括(如屬註冊為擔保有限公司的公司)有關聲明擔保款額的決議，均須按同樣方式及在附有同樣附帶條件的情況下當作是該公司的條件及規例，猶如該公司若已根據本條例成立則須加入其章程大綱內的該等條件及規例已載於經註冊的章程大綱內，而其餘的條件及規例則已載於經註冊的章程細則內一樣。
4	Subsection (1) shall not be construed as- (a) limiting the application of any other provision in the Amending Ordinance; or (b) validating any transaction, entered into before the commencement of sections 5A and 5B, which would have been void **if** not for the enactment of those sections.	第(1)款不得解釋為— (a) 限制修訂條例中任何其他條文的適用範圍；或 (b) 使在第5A及5B條生效前達成的且若非因該等條文的訂立而本已屬無效的任何交易變成有效。
5	Particulars of the total amount of the indebtedness of the company in respect of all mortgages and charges which are required to be registered with the Registrar under this Ordinance, or which would have been required so to be registered **if** created after 1 January 1912.	該公司負債總額詳情，而該等負債乃有關所有根據本條例所規定須向處長登記的按揭及押記者，或所有若於1912年1月1日後設定則須如此登記的按揭或押記者。
6	Where a company acquires any property which is subject to a charge of any such kind as would, **if** it had been created by the company after the acquisition of the property, have been required to be registered under this Part, the company shall cause the particulars of the charge (which must include those specified in section 80(1A) and be in the specified form), together with a copy (certified in the prescribed manner to be a correct copy) of the instrument, if any, by which the charge was created or is evidenced, to be delivered to the Registrar for registration in manner required by this Ordinance within 5 weeks after the date on which the acquisition is completed.	凡公司獲取任何受某項押記所規限的財產，而該押記是屬於一種若在公司收購財產後始設定即鬚根據本部登記的押記，則公司須在完成獲取該財產的日期後5個星期內，安排將該項押記的詳情(該等詳情須包括第80(1A)條所指明的詳情並須以指明格式述明)，連同設定或證明該項押記的任何文書(如有的話)的副本一份(經按訂明方式核證為正確副本)，以本條例所規定的方式交付處長登記。
7	Where a series of debentures containing, or giving by reference to any other instrument, any charge to the benefit of which the debenture holders of that series are entitled pari passu is created by a company, it shall for the purposes of this section be sufficient **if** there are delivered to or received by the Registrar within 5 weeks after the execution of the deed containing the charge or, if there is no such deed, after the execution of any debentures of the series, the following particulars-…	凡公司設定一系列債權證，而該等債權證包含任何押記或藉提述任何其他文書而給予任何押記，並且由該系列債權證的持有人同等享有該項押記的利益，則若於載有該項押記的契據簽立後5個星期內，或(如無上述契據)於該系列任何債權證簽立後5個星期內，將下述詳情交付處長或由處長接獲，就本條而言，乃屬足夠—……

Table 4.6 'If' translated as '倘' (tǎng) or '倘若' (tǎng ruò)

No.	*English original*	*Chinese translation*
1	**If** any such money is not so repaid within 38 days after the issue of the prospectus, the directors of the company shall be jointly and severally liable to repay that money with interest at the rate of 8 per cent per annum from the expiration of the 38th day.	**倘**在招股章程發出後38天內，仍有任何該等款項未如此退還，則該公司的董事須共同及各別負法律責任，將該等款項連同由第38天屆滿時開始按年息8厘計算的利息退還。
2	In reckoning for the purposes of this section and section 44B the 3rd or 5th day after another day, any intervening day which is a Saturday or Sunday or which is a general holiday in Hong Kong shall be disregarded, and **if** the 3rd or 5th day (as so reckoned) is itself a Saturday or Sunday or such a holiday there shall for the said purposes be substituted the 1st day thereafter which is none of them.	就本條及第44B條而言，計算某一日期後的第3天或第5天時，在有關期間內出現的星期六或星期日或香港公眾假日，均不予計算；**倘**如此計算出來的第3天或第5天本身是星期六或星期日或香港公眾假日，則就上述兩條條文而言，須以隨後而並非是星期六或星期日或香港公眾假日的第一日取代。
3	Where the permission has not been applied for as aforesaid, or has been refused as aforesaid, the company shall forthwith repay without interest all money received from applicants in pursuance the prospectus, and, **if** any such money is not repaid within 8 days after the company becomes liable to repay it, the directors of the company shall be jointly and severally liable to repay that money with interest at the rate of 8 per cent per annum from the expiration of the 8th day.	凡未有如前述般提出批准申請，或有關批准已如前述般被拒絕，公司須立即將依據招股章程從申請人收到的所有款-項，全數無息退還申請人；**倘若**在該公司有法律責任退還款項後8 天內，仍有任何該等款項並未退還，則該公司的董事須共同及各別負法律責任，將該等款項連同由第8天屆滿時開始按年息8厘計算的利息退還。

However, if the second sentence is changed to '**如**如此計算出來的第3天或第5天本身是星期六或星期日或香港公眾假日,' it may sound slightly awkward due to the repetition of '如' (rú), but this is only a matter of expression in the Chinese language and does not affect the function of the translation.

(V) 'If' translated as '在 …… 時' (zài …… shí)

There are eight sentences in which 'if' is translated as '在 …… 時' (zài …… shí), as shown in Table 4.7.

In these eight sentences, 'if' is translated as '在 …… 時' (zài …… shí; at the time of) in Chinese. However, in sentences No. 1, 5, and 7, 'if' is preceded by introductory words such as 'if,' 'where,' or 'in a case.' Therefore, to avoid repetition, 'if' in these sentences is translated as '在 …… 時' (zài …… shí) instead of '如' (rú). For example, in sentence No. 1, the conditional clause 'if successful in his defence' is translated as '在被告人勝訴時' instead of '如被告人勝訴' because the word 'if' has already been used earlier in the sentence to introduce another conditional clause 'if it appears by credible testimony that.' In the English original text, the second 'if' clause is subordinate to the first 'if' clause and is placed at the end of the sentence. However, in Chinese, conditional clauses are usually located at the beginning of the sentence. Therefore, if we translate the sentence as '如依據可信證供而覺得有理由相信如被告人勝訴,' it would be unnatural due to the repeated use of '如' (rú) in the same sentence. The same rationale also applies to sentences No. 5 and 7, in which 'where' and 'in a case' are translated as '如' (rú), and 'if' is translated as '在 …… 時' (zài …… shí) to avoid repetition.

In addition, in sentences No. 2, 4, and 8, 'if' is translated as '在 …… 時' (zài …… shí) because they contain time-related words in the context. For example, in sentence No. 2, 'if it is shown that, at the time the guarantee was entered into or the security provided,' 'at the time' refers to a specific time period. Similarly, in sentence No. 4, 'if the relevant property was not in Hong Kong at the time the charge was created by the company,' 'at the time' again refers to a specific time period. In sentence No. 8, 'if such payment was made during a period of 4 months before the commencement of the winding up', 'during a period of 4 months' refers to a specific time period as well. Therefore, it seems more appropriate to translate 'if' in these sentences as '在 …… 時' (zài …… shí) even though such translation weakens the meaning of 'if' as a condition. But the translation does not affect the reader's understanding and keeps the same function as the original text.

Actually, '在 …… 時' (zài …… shí) in sentences No. 3 and 6 can be replaced with '如' (rú) without causing any ambiguity. For example, in sentence No. 3, '在顧及有關個案的所有情況而認為恰當時' can also be expressed as '如顧及有關個案的所有情況而認為恰當.'

(VI) 'If' translated as '在 …… 情況下' (zài …… qíng kuàng xià)

There are a total of 26 sentences in which 'if' is translated as '在 …… 情況下' (zài …… qíng kuàng xià), as shown in Table 4.8.

Table 4.7 'If' translated as '在 …… 時' (zài …… shí)

No.	*English original*	*Chinese translation*
1	Where a limited company is plaintiff in any action or other legal proceeding, any judge having jurisdiction in the matter may, if it appears by credible testimony that there is reason to believe that the company will be unable to pay the costs of the defendant **if** successful in his defence, require sufficient security to be given for those costs, and may stay all proceedings until the security is given.	凡一間有限公司在任何訴訟或其他法律程序中為原告人，任何在有關事宜上具有司法管轄權的法官，如依據可信證供而覺得有理由相信**在**被告人勝訴**時**，該公司將無力支付被告人的訟費，則該法官可規定該公司須就該等訟費給予充分保證，並可擱置所有法律程序，直至該公司給予該項保證為止。
2	Subsection (2)- (a) shall not apply to a guarantee entered into or any security provided by the company in connection with a loan or quasi-loan made by any person to, or a credit transaction entered into by any person as creditor for, a person who is not a director of the company or of its holding company **if** it is shown that, at the time the guarantee was entered into or the security provided, the person to whom the guarantee was given or the security provided, as the case may be, did not know the relevant circumstances; and…	第(2)款— (a) 並不適用於公司就一項由任何人向一名並非該公司或其控股公司的董事的人作出的貸款或類似貸款或一項由任何人以債權人身分為該人訂立的信貸交易而訂立的擔保或提供的任何保證，但前提是須證明**在**訂立該項擔保或提供該項保證**時**，獲給予該項擔保或獲提供該項保證(視屬何情況而定)的人不知悉有關情況；及……
3	Where a company has passed a resolution authorizing the issue of shares at a discount, it may apply to the court for an order sanctioning the issue, and on any such application the court, **if**, having regard to all the circumstances of the case, it thinks proper so to do, may make an order sanctioning the issue on such terms and conditions as it thinks fit.	凡公司已通過決議批准按折扣發行股份，可向法院申請一項命令認許該次發行，而法院應上述申請，**在**顧及有關個案的所有情況而認為恰當**時**，可按其認為合適的條款及條件，作出命令認許該次發行。
4	Notwithstanding subsection (1), this Part does not extend to charges on property in Hong Kong of a non-Hong Kong company registered under Part XI **if** the relevant property was not in Hong Kong at the time the charge was created by the company, or at the time it was acquired by the company subsequent to the creation of the charge.	儘管有第(1)款的規定，根據第XI部註冊的非香港公司位於香港的財產如符合以下描述，則本部的適用範圍不擴及該財產的押記：**在**該公司設定該押記**時**，或在該公司於該押記設定後獲取該財產時，該財產不是位於香港。

(*Continued*)

Table 4.7 (Continued)

No.	*English original*	*Chinese translation*
5	Where the Registrar enters a memorandum of satisfaction in whole under subsection (1), he shall, **if** required and upon payment of the prescribed fee, endorse the words 'satisfaction entered' or the expression in Chinese '已清償' upon the instrument creating the charge.	如處長根據第(1)款記入有關全部債項的清償備忘錄，則**在**有要求提出**時**及獲支付訂明費用後，須在設定該項-押記的文書上註明'satisfaction entered'或'已清償'字樣。
6	On a poll taken at a meeting of a company or a meeting of any class of members of a company, a member entitled to more than 1 vote need not, **if** he votes, use all his votes or cast all the votes he uses in the same way.	在公司會議上或在公司的任何類別成員的會議上以投票方式表決時，有權投多於1票的成員**在**表決**時**，無須使用其所有的票，或以同一方式全數投其使用的票。
7	Section 47A does not prohibit an unlisted company from giving financial assistance in a case where the acquisition of shares in question is or was an acquisition of shares in the company or, **if** it is a subsidiary of another unlisted company, in that other company if the following provisions of this section, and sections 47F to 48, are complied with as respects the giving of that assistance.	如**在**給予資助方面本條下列條文及第47F至48條的條文獲遵從，而所涉及的股份收購在現時或以前是一項非上市公司的股份收購，或該非上市公司是另一間非上市公司的附屬公司**時**，所涉及的股份收購在現時或以前是一項該另一間非上市公司的股份收購，則第47A條並不禁止非上市公司在上述情況下給予資助。
8	Payment from the Protection of Wages on Insolvency Fund under section 18 of the Protection of Wages on Insolvency Ordinance (Cap 380) to any clerk or servant in respect of wages or salary or both in respect of services rendered to the company **if** such payment was made during a period of 4 months before the commencement of the winding up.	根據《破產欠薪保障條例》(第380章)第18條，就任何文員或受僱人向公司提供服務而應得的工資及薪金或兩者之一，**在**清盤開始前4個月期間內，從破產欠薪保障基金撥付的款項。

Table 4.8 'If' translated as '在 …… 情況下' (zài …… qíng kuàng xià)

No.	*English original*	*Chinese translation*
1	Where a document is required to be delivered to the Registrar under any provision of this Ordinance, the Registrar may, **if** he thinks fit, accept the information in question in any form approved by him.	凡任何文件根據本條例的條文須交付處長，處長可**在**他認為適當的**情況下**，接受采用經他批准的任何形式的有關資料。
2	Except as provided in subsections (9) and (10), this section shall not require the inclusion in accounts prepared by a company that is, or is the holding company of, an authorized financial institution of particulars of- (a) …; (b) …; or (c) …, **if**, but only if, either of the following conditions is satisfied- (i) …; or…	除第(9)及(10)款另有規定外，就任何本身是一間認可財務機構或是一間認可財務機構的控股公司的公司而言，在其中一項有關條件符合，並只有**在**其中一項有關條件符合的**情況下**，本條並不規定其擬備的帳目須載有下述詳情— (a) ……； (b) ……；或 (c) ……， 而上述有關條件為— (i) ……；或……
3	Without prejudice to any liability imposed on directors of companies otherwise than by this subsection, a director of a company that has entered into a transaction or arrangement in contravention of section 157H shall be liable- (a) …; and (b)…, **if**- (i) …; (ii) …; or (iii) …	在不損害本款以外的規定所施加於公司董事的任何法律責任下，如某間公司在違反第157H條的情況下訂立一項交易或安排，**在**符合有關說明的**情況下**，該公司的董事須— (a) ……；及 (b) ……， 上述有關說明指— (i) ……； (ii) ……；或 (iii) ……
4	Where a listed company's relevant financial documents or summary financial report are or is treated as being sent to an entitled person of the company by virtue of the operation of subsection (1), the documents or report, as the case may be, shall be treated as being sent to the person not less than 21 days before the date of the general meeting to which the documents or report, as the case may be, relate or relates **if** and only if- (a) …; and (b) …	凡上市公司的有關財務文件或財務摘要報告憑藉第(1)款的施行視為已送交該公司的某有權利的人，則在以下情況下並只**在**以下**情況下**，該等文件或報告(視屬何情況而定)須視為在與該等文件或報告(視屬何情況而定)有關的大會舉行的日期前不少於21天已送交該人— (a) ……；及 (b) ……

(*Continued*)

Table 4.8 (Continued)

No.	English original	Chinese translation
5	For the purposes of this section a person is connected with a director of a company **if**, but only if, he is- (a) …; or (b)…; or (c) …; or (d) …	就本條而言，如在下述情況及只**在**下述**情況**，某人始與一名公司董事有關連— (a) ……；或 (b) ……；或 (c) ……；或 (d) ……
6	For the purposes of this section, a person is connected with a director of a company **if**, but only if, he is- (a) …; (b) …; or (c) …	就本條而言，任何人**在**下述的**情況下**即屬(並僅在下述情況下方屬)與公司的一名董事有關連— (a) ……； (b) ……；或 (c) ……
7	The nomination of a person as a reserve director of a private company ceases to be valid **if**- (a) before the death of the director in respect of whom he was nominated- (i) he resigns as reserve director in accordance with section 157D; or (ii) the company in general meeting revokes the nomination; or (b) the director in respect of whom he was nominated ceases to be the sole member and sole director of the company for any reason other than the death of that director.	凡任何人被提名為私人公司的備任董事，該提名**在**以下**情況**出現時即不再有效— (a) 如在該人的提名所關乎的董事去世前— (i) 該人按照第157D條的規定，辭去備任董事職位；或 (ii) 該公司在大會上撤銷該提名；或 (b) 如該人的提名所關乎的董事因任何理由(該董事去世除外)不再是該公司的唯一成員及唯一董事。
8	For the purposes of subsection (4), the composition of a company's board of directors shall be deemed to be controlled by another company if that other company by the exercise of some power exercisable by it, without the consent of any other person, can appoint or remove all or a majority of the directors, and, for the purposes of this provision, that other company shall be deemed to have power to make such an appointment **if**- (a) …; or (b) …	就第(4)款而言，一間公司如在無需他人同意下，可藉行使若干可由其行使的權力，委任另一間公司的全數或過半數的董事或將其免任，則該另一間公司的董事局的組合，須當作受該公司所控制，而就本條文而言，**在**以下**情況**，該公司須當作有作出上述委任的權力— (a) ……；或 (b) ……

9	Subsection (4) does not apply **<u>if</u>**- (a) the terms provided for the redemption or purchase to take place at a date later than that of the commencement of the winding up; or (b) during the period beginning with the date on which the redemption or purchase was to have taken place and ending with the commencement of the winding up the company could not at any time have lawfully made a distribution equal in value to the price at which the shares were to have been redeemed or purchased.	第(4)款不適用於以下**情況—** (a) 如有關條款訂定贖回或購買股份的日期是在清盤開始的日期之後；或 (b) 公司在須贖回或購買股份的日期起至清盤開始之日的一段期間內，假若不能在任何時候合法地作出價值與須予贖回或購買的股份價格相等的分發。
10	In the event of non-compliance with or contravention of any of the requirements of this section, a director or other person responsible for the prospectus shall not incur any liability by reason of the non-compliance or contravention, **<u>if</u>**- (a) …; or (b) …; or (c) …	如本條任何規定不獲遵從或被違反，董事或其他對招股章程負責的人**在**下列**情況下**，不會因有關規定不獲遵從或被違反而招致任何法律責任**—** (a) ……；或 (b) ……；或 (c) ……
11	A special resolution to confer, vary, revoke or renew authority under subsection (3) is not effective **<u>if</u>** any member of the company holding shares to which the resolution relates exercises the voting rights carried by any of those shares in voting on the resolution and the resolution would not have been passed if he had not done so and for this purpose- (a) …; (b) …; and (c) …	根據第(3)款授予、更改、撤銷或重訂權限的特別決議，**在**下述**情況中**並無效力：持有與該項決議有關的股份的公司成員，行使該等股份所附有的表決權，就該項決議進行表決，而假若該等成員不曾如此表決，則該項決議不會獲通過，並且就此而言**—** (a) ……； (b) ……；及 (c) ……
12	Subsection (1) shall not require the disclosure by a company which carries on business outside Hong Kong of information with respect to the undertaking regarded by the directors as being the company's ultimate parent undertaking **<u>if</u>**— (a) the disclosure would, in their opinion, be harmful to the business of that parent undertaking or of the company or any other of that parent undertaking's subsidiaries; and (b) the Financial Secretary agrees that the information need not be disclosed.	**在**以下說明均符合的**情況下**，第(1)款並不規定在香港以外經營業務的公司須就董事視為該公司最終母企業的企業作出資料披露— (a) 該公司的董事認為，上述資料披露會對該母企業或該公司或該母企業的任何其他附屬公司的業務不利；及 (b) 財政司司長同意該項資料無需披露。

(*Continued*)

Table 4.8 (Continued)

No.	*English original*	*Chinese translation*
13	Subject to sections 141CC(1) and 141CE(1), for the purposes of proviso (b)(iv) to subsection (1), a copy of a summary financial report of a listed company shall be treated as having been duly sent **if**- (a) …; (b) …	在不抵觸第141CC(1)及141CE(1)條的情況下，就第(1)款但書的(b)(iv)段而言，上市公司的財務摘要報告**在**以下**情況**須視為已妥善地送交— (a) ……； (b) ……
14	The court may only make an order under subsection (1) **if** it is satisfied that— (a) the application is made in good faith; and (b) the inspection applied for is for a proper purpose.	法院**在**信納以下事項的**情況下**，方可根據第(1)款作出命令— (a) 有關申請是真誠作出的；及 (b) 所申請的查閱，是為了一項屬恰當的目的。
15	An unregistered company shall, for the purposes of this Ordinance, be deemed to be unable to pay its debts- (a) **if** …; (b) **if** …; (c) **if** …; (d) **if** …	就本條例而言，如有以下**情況**，非註冊公司須當作無能力償付其債項— (a) ……； (b) ……； (c) ……； (d) ……
16	Subsection (1) shall not require the disclosure of information **if**- (c) the disclosure would, in the opinion of the directors of that other undertaking, be harmful to the business of that other undertaking or of any of its subsidiaries; and (d) the Financial Secretary agrees that the information need not be disclosed.	**在**以下說明均符合的**情況下**，第(1)款並不規定須就該企業作出資料披露— (c) 該另一企業的董事認為披露有關資料會對該另一企業或其任何附屬公司的業務不利；及 (d) 財政司司長同意該項資料無需披露。
17	Subsections (1) and (2) shall not apply to a company's profit and loss account **if**- (a) the company has subsidiaries; and (b) the profit and loss account is framed as a consolidated profit and loss account dealing with all or any of the company's subsidiaries as well as the company	第(1)及(2)款**在**以下**情況**下不適用於公司的損益表— (a) 公司有附屬公司；及 (b) 該損益表是以綜合損益表的形式擬定，處理公司本身及公司的所有或任何附屬公司。
18	A meeting of a company shall, notwithstanding that it is called by shorter notice than that specified in subsection (2) or in the company's articles, as the case may be, be deemed to have been duly called **if** it is so agreed- (a) …; and (b) …	公司的會議，即使其召開的通知期短於第(2)款或公司的章程細則(視屬何情況而定)所指明者，**在**下述**情況下**仍須當作已妥為召開— (a) ……；及 (b) ……

19	A company is not required to hold a meeting in accordance with subsection (1) **if**- (a) everything that is required or intended to be done at the meeting (by resolution or otherwise) is done by a resolution or resolutions in accordance with section 116B; and (b) a copy of each document (including any accounts or records) which under this Ordinance would be required to be laid before the company at the meeting or otherwise produced at the meeting is provided to each member of the company- (i) …; and (ii) …	**在**符合下述**條件下**，公司無須按照第(1)款舉行會議— (a) 所有須在或擬在會議上(藉決議或其他方式)作出的事情，已藉按照第116B條通過的決議作出；及 (b) 因根據本條例規定須在會議上提交公司省覽或有其他原由而須在會議上交出的每份文件(包括任何帳目或紀錄)均— (i) ……；並且 (ii) ……
20	The court may only make an order about costs (including the requirement as to indemnification) under this section in favour of the member **if** it is satisfied that the member was acting in good faith in, and had reasonable grounds for, making the application, or bringing or intervening in the proceedings.	法院在信納成員**在**作出申請或提起或介入法律程序時是真誠行事和具合理理由如此行事的**情況下**，方可根據本條就訟費(包括關於彌償的規定)作出有利於該成員的命令。
21	This section shall not require the inclusion in accounts of particulars of any loan or quasi-loan made by a company or a subsidiary thereof to, or any credit transaction entered into by a company or a subsidiary thereof as creditor for, an employee of the company or subsidiary, as the case may be, **if**- (a) …; (b) …; (c) …; and (d) ...	**在**下述**情況下**，本條並不規定將有關某公司或其附屬公司向該公司或附屬公司(視屬何情況而定)的一名僱員作出的任何貸款或類似貸款或某公司或其附屬公司以債權人身分為該公司或附屬公司(視屬何情況而定)的一名僱員訂立的任何信貸交易的詳情載於帳目內— (a) ……; (b) ……; (c) ……; 及 (d) ……
22	A listed company shall not send any copy of a summary financial report to an entitled person of the company in place of a copy of the relevant financial documents- (a) **if** the memorandum or articles of association of the company does not permit the company to do that; (b) **if** the person is a holder of debentures of the company and the instrument that constitutes or governs the debentures does not permit the company to do that; or (c) **if** an order under section 141CG would thereby be contravened.	**在**以下**情況下**，上市公司不得向該公司的某有權利的人送交財務摘要報告以代替有關財務文件— (a) 公司的章程大綱或組織章程細則並不准許公司如此行事； (b) 該人是該公司的債權證持有人，而構成或規管該債權證的文書並不准許該公司如此行事；或 (c) 如此行事則會違反第141CG條所指的命令。

(*Continued*)

Table 4.8 (Continued)

No.	*English original*	*Chinese translation*
23	Whether or not a request referred to in subsection (1) has been made, the Commission may, by notice published in the Gazette, and subject to such conditions (if any) as the Commission thinks fit and specified in the notice, exempt- (a) any class of companies; or (b) any class of prospectuses issued by companies, from any or all of the requirements of the relevant provisions **if**, having regard to the circumstances, the Commission considers that the exemption will not prejudice the interest of the investing public and compliance with any or all of those requirements, in the case of that class of companies or prospectuses, as the case may be- (c) would be irrelevant or unduly burdensome; or (d) is otherwise unnecessary or inappropriate.	不論是否已有第(1)款提述的請求提出，監察委員會可藉在憲報刊登的公告並在它認為合適的在該公告指明的條件(如有的話)規限下，豁免— (a) 某類公司；或 (b) 公司發出的某類招股章程， 使其無需符合任何或所有有關條文的規定，但該項豁免只可**在**下述**情況下**作出：監察委員會於顧及有關情況後，認為該項豁免並不會損害投資大眾的利益，而要求該類公司或該類招股章程(視屬何情況而定)符合任何或所有該等規定— (c) 會是不相干的或會構成不適當的負擔；或 (d) 在其他情況下是無需要或不適當的。
24	Where it is proposed to offer any shares in or debentures of a company incorporated outside Hong Kong (whether the company has or has not established a place of business in Hong Kong) to the public by a prospectus or class of prospectuses issued generally, there may, on the request of the applicant, and subject to such conditions (if any) as the Commission thinks fit, be issued by the Commission a certificate of exemption from compliance with any or all of the requirements of the relevant provisions **if**, having regard to the circumstances, the Commission considers that the exemption will not prejudice the interest of the investing public and compliance with any or all of those requirements- (a) …; or (b) …	凡擬藉公開發出招股章程或某類招股章程而將某間在香港以外成立為法團的公司(不論該公司已否在香港設立營業地點)的股份或債權證向公眾作出要約，監察委員會可應申請人的請求並在它認為合適的條件(如有的話)規限下，發出豁免證明書，豁免上述招股章程使其無需符合任何或所有有關條文的規定，但該項豁免只可**在**下述**情況下**作出：監察委員會於顧及有關情況後，認為該項豁免並不會損害投資大眾的利益，而要求上述招股章程符合任何或所有該等規定— (a) ……；或 (b) ……
25	In the event of non-compliance with or contravention of any of the requirements imposed by subsection (1)(a) and (b), a director or other person responsible for the prospectus shall not incur any liability by reason of the non-compliance or contravention, **if**- (a) …; or (b) …; or (c) … A company shall be deemed to be unable to pay its debts- (a) **if** …; or (b) **if** …; or (c) **if** …	如第(1)(a)及(b)款所訂的任何規定不獲遵從或被違反，董事或其他對招股章程負責的人**在**下列**情況下**，不會因有關規定不獲遵從或被違反而招致任何法律責任— (a) ……；或 (b) ……；或 (c) …… 如有以下**情況**，公司須當作無能力償付其債項— (a) ……；或 (b) ……；或 (c) ……

This translation mainly refers to the case when 'if' introduces multiple conditional clauses. If such conditional clauses introduced by 'if' adopt a digital table format (referring to the case of many clauses of parallel relationship often occurring in legal provisions, generally expressed by Arabic numbers 1, 2, 3 or Latin letters a, b, c), there are usually two translation methods: (1) using the same digital table format by following the original sentence structure; (2) using such expressions as 'in the following cases or under the following circumstances' before listing each case or circumstance. Sentences No. 2–26 use the second method. In these sentences, 'if' introduces two or more conditional clauses, and the phrase 'in the following cases' or similar phrases are added before each condition is described, so as to give readers a rough idea of what is to be expressed. For example, in sentences No. 15, 22, and 26, 'if' appears at the beginning of each conditional clause repeatedly. In such an English expression, there is no big difference between placing 'if' before each conditional clause and using 'if' only once. The latter expression is also very common in legal provisions. Therefore, the translation for these sentences adds 'in the following cases' before each conditional clause and then translates each condition separately. However, sentence No. 1 is an exception, because 'if' is not used to introduce multiple conditions. So its translation can be changed to a more concise expression: '**如**處長認為適當，可接受采用經他批准的任何形式的有關資料。'

(VII) 'If' with no translation

There are a total of 26 sentences in which 'if' is not translated, as shown in Table 4.9.

In these sentences, 'if' is obviously used as the introductory word for conditional sentences in the original, indicating a hypothetical situation, which is however not reflected in the translation. There are two situations:

(1) When two introductory words for conditional clauses appear in one sentence, such as the simultaneous occurrence of two 'ifs' (as in sentence No. 12), of 'in the case' and 'if' (as in sentences No. 3, 5, 11, 14), or of 'where' and 'if' (as in sentences No. 1, 2, 9, 20). In these cases, the second 'if' as the second introductory word for conditional clauses is untranslated, though it can still be translated. For example, sentence No. 13 can be translated as '**如**公司有核數師，則.' Although an untranslated 'if' significantly reduces its meaning as an introductory word for conditional sentences, it does not affect the reader's understanding, so it can still be considered to have achieved the same function as the original text.
(2) 'If' is not translated, but for the sake of internal coherence, conjunctions indicating contrast such as '而' (ér; but) or '但' (dàn; but) are added, as in sentences No. 4, 5, 9, 11, 12, 13, 14, 17, 18, 25, and 26, or conjunctions indicating progression such as '並且' (bìng qiě; and) or '而且' (ér qiě; and), as in sentences No. 22 and 23. However, in these sentences, 'if' can actually be translated as '如' (rú). For example, sentence No. 26 can be translated as '如招股章程符合(a)段第(i)、(ii)、(iii)及(iv)節的規定，則處長須註冊該招股章程。'

Table 4.9 'If' with no translation

No.	*English original*	*Chinese translation*
1	**<u>If</u>**, where the prospectus includes a statement purporting to be made by an expert, he has not given, or has before delivery of the prospectus for registration withdrawn, his written consent to the issue of the prospectus with the statement included in the form and context in which it is included or there does not appear in the prospectus a statement that he has given and has not withdrawn his consent as aforesaid.	凡招股章程載有一項看來是由一名專家作出的陳述，而該名專家未有給予書面同意，同意發出一份載有一項在形式和文意上一如所載的陳述的招股章程，或在該份招股章程交付註冊前已撤回其書面同意，或在該招股章程內並未載有一項陳述，說明該名專家已給予前述的同意及未有將其撤回。
2	**<u>If</u>** where a company is wound up it is shown that proper books of account were not kept by the company throughout the period of 2 years immediately preceding the commencement of the winding up, or the period between the incorporation of the company and the commencement of the winding up, whichever is the shorter, every officer of the company who is in default shall, unless he shows that he acted honestly and that in the circumstances in which the business of the company was carried on the default was excusable, be guilty of an offence and liable to imprisonment and a fine.	凡公司被清盤，而有證明顯示公司在緊接其清盤開始前的2年的整段期間或在其成立為法團至其開始清盤的整段期間(兩者以較短的期間為準)內，並無備存妥善的帳簿，則公司的每名失責高級人員，除非能證明自己是誠實行事，而該項失責在公司業務的經營情況下是可予寬宥的，否則即屬犯罪，可處監禁及罰款。
3	Provided that, in the case of a banking company which has branch banks beyond the limits of Hong Kong, it shall be sufficient (subject to the powers of the auditors under subsections (4) and (6)) **<u>if</u>** the auditor is allowed access to such copies and extracts from such books and accounts of any such branch as have been transmitted to the head office of the company in Hong Kong.	但如公司為一間銀行公司，且在香港境外設有分行，則(在不抵觸核數師根據第(4)及(6)款所具權力的情況下)核數師只要獲准取用該等分行傳轉至該公司在香港的總辦事處的簿冊和帳目的副本及摘錄，已屬足夠。

4	The inspector may, and, **<u>if</u>** so directed by the Financial Secretary, shall, make interim reports to the Financial Secretary, and on the conclusion of the investigation shall make a final report to the Financial Secretary.	審查員可以，而在財政司司長有所指示下則須，向財政司司長作出中期報告；審查員並須於調查完結後向財政司司長作出最後報告。
5	In the case of any property, **<u>if</u>** the order so directs, freed from any charge which is by virtue of the compromise or arrangement to cease to have effect.	如屬任何財產，而該項命令又有所指示，該財產須不再受憑藉此項妥協或債務償還安排而停止生效的押記所規限。
6	**<u>If</u>** a person acts in contravention of a disqualification order, he is guilty of an offence and is liable to imprisonment and a fine.	任何人違反一項取消資格令，即屬犯罪，可處監禁及罰款。
7	A person is personally responsible for all the relevant debts of a company **<u>if</u>** at any time- (a) in contravention of a disqualification order or of section 156 he is involved in the management of the company; or (b) as a person who is involved in the management of the company, he acts or is willing to act on instructions given without the leave of the court by a person whom he knows at that time to be the subject of a disqualification order or to be an undischarged bankrupt.	任何人— (a) 違反一項取消資格令或違反第156條而牽涉於公司的管理；或 (b) 作為牽涉於該公司的管理的人，如按或願意按另一人在未經法院許可的情況下所發出的指示行事，而該人當時知道該另一人是一項取消資格令所指的人或是一名未獲解除破產的破產人，須對該公司一切有關債項承擔個人責任。
8	A company which was incorporated before the commencement of the Companies (Amendment) Ordinance 1984 (6 of 1984) and which has such an official seal as is mentioned in subsection (1) may use the seal for sealing such securities and documents as are there mentioned notwithstanding anything in any instrument constituting or regulating the company or in any instrument made before such commencement which relates to any securities or documents **<u>if</u>** they are sealed with that seal.	一間公司如在《1984年公司(修訂)條例》+(1984年第6號)生效前成立為法團，並且備有第(1)款所述的正式印章，可使用該印章在該款所述的證券及文件上蓋印，而不論在任何組成或規管該公司的文書中有任何規定，亦不論在該條例生-效前所訂立任何關於蓋上該印章的證券或文件的文書中有任何規定。

(Continued)

Table 4.9 (Continued)

No.	*English original*	*Chinese translation*
9	Subject to subsection (4), where an application is made to a company under this section for a new certificate, the company shall, **<u>if</u>** it intends to issue such certificate under this section, publish a notice in the specified form advertising its intention to do so, as follows-…	在第(4)款的規限下，凡有人根據本條向公司申請發出新股票，而公司亦擬根據本條發出此股票，則公司須刊登一項具指明格式的公告以發表其意向，公告如下—……
10	**<u>If</u>** and so far as is necessary, alter its memorandum by reducing the amount of its share capital and of its shares accordingly.	並且於必需時，可藉減少其股本額及股份數額而據此修改其章程大綱。
11	In the case of a company having a share capital **<u>if</u>** there has been no change in the matters required to be contained in a return, since the date of the last return, the company may in lieu of the return required by subsection (1), make a return by certificate in the specified form.	如有關公司屬有股本公司，而自最近一份申報表的日期後，規定必須載於申報表的事項並無任何改變，則該公司可藉提交一份具有指明格式的證明書作出申報，以代替第(1)款所規定的申報表。
12	Neither subsection (1) nor subsection (2) shall require the disclosure by a company of information with respect to another body corporate if that other body is incorporated outside Hong Kong or, being incorporated in Hong Kong, carries on business outside Hong Kong **<u>if</u>** the disclosure would, in the opinion of the directors of the company, be harmful to the business of the company or of that other body and the Financial Secretary agrees that the information need not be disclosed.	如該另一法人團體在香港以外成立，或在香港成立而在香港以外經營業務，而公司的董事認為披露有關該法人團體的資料會對公司或對該法人團體的業務不利，且財政司司長亦同意該等資料無須予以披露，則第(1) 或(2)款及第(2)款並不規定公司須作上述披露。
13	He shall, **<u>if</u>** the company has auditors, secure that a copy of the resolution is sent to them, or that they are otherwise notified of its contents, at or before the time the resolution is supplied to a member for signature.	而公司是有核數師的，則該名董事或秘書須確保在提供該項建議的決議予成員簽署之時或之前，將其文本送予該核數師，或以其他方式使核數師獲悉其內容。
14	For the purposes of this section, the directors shall, in the case of a meeting at which a resolution is to be proposed as a special resolution, be deemed not to have duly convened the meeting **<u>if</u>** they do not give such notice thereof as is required by section 116.	就本條而言，如某項決議擬在某次會議上以特別決議的形式提出，而董事沒有發出第116條所規定的會議通知書，則董事須當作並未妥為召開會議。

15	In any other case, it shall be the duty of the holding company, **<u>if</u>** required by its auditors to do so, to take all such steps as are reasonably open to it to obtain from the subsidiary such information and explanation as aforesaid.	在任何其他情況下，控股公司有責任應其核數師的要求，採取一切合理可行的步驟，從該附屬公司取得上述的資料及解釋。
16	A company which, at or after the commencement of the Companies (Amendment) Ordinance 1984 (6 of 1984), is registered as unlimited may be re-registered as limited **<u>if</u>** a special resolution that it should be so re-registered (complying with the requirement of subsection (2)) is passed and an application in that behalf, framed in the specified form and signed by a director or by the secretary of the company, is lodged with the Registrar together with the documents mentioned in subsection (3) not earlier than the day on which the copy of the resolution forwarded to him in pursuance of section 117 is received by him.	在《1984年公司(修訂)條例》+(1984年第6號)生效時或之後註冊的無限公司，可藉以下方式重新註冊為有限公司，即一項決定公司應如此重新登記的特別決議(此決議須符合第(2)款的規定)獲得通過，並按指明格式為此擬定作出有關申請，申請書由一名董事或公司秘書籤署，連同第(3)款所述的文件，在不早於處長收到公司依據第117條將決議文本遞送予處長之日提交處長。
17	This section shall not prevent a subsidiary which is a member of its holding company from accepting and holding further shares in its holding company **<u>if</u>** such further shares are allotted to it as fully paid up in consequence of a capitalization of reserves or profits by such holding company.	本條並不阻止一間作為其控股公司成員的附屬公司，接受及持有更多其控股公司的股份，但該等股份須是該控股公司在將儲備或利潤資本化後，作為全部繳足股款的股份分配予該附屬公司的。
18	**<u>If</u>** any person acts in contravention of subsection (1), he shall be liable to a fine.	任何人違反第(1)款，可處罰款。
19	The Registrar shall register a prospectus **<u>if</u>** subparagraphs (i), (ii), (iii) and (iv) of paragraph (a) are complied with in respect of that prospectus.	處長須將招股章程註冊，但該招股章程須符合(a)段第(i)、(ii)、(iii)及(iv)節的規定。
20	Where a person making an offer to which this section relates is a company or a firm, it shall be sufficient **<u>if</u>** the document aforesaid is signed on behalf of the company or firm by 2 directors of the company or not less than half of the partners, as the case may be, and any such director or partner may sign by his agent authorized in writing.	凡作出與本條有關的要約的人是一間公司或商號，則上述文件只須由該公司2名董事或不少於半數的合夥人代表該公司或商號(視屬何情況而定)簽署，即屬足夠，而該等董事或合夥人亦可由其以書面授權的代理人代為簽署。

(Continued)

Table 4.9 (Continued)

No.	*English original*	*Chinese translation*
21	For purposes of subsection (2), a member who holds such shares is to be regarded as exercising the voting rights carried by them in voting on the resolution not only **<u>if</u>** he votes in respect of them on a poll on the question whether the resolution shall be passed, but also **<u>if</u>** he votes on the resolution otherwise than on a poll; and, notwithstanding anything in a company's articles, any member of the company may demand a poll on that question.	就第(2)款而言，持有該等股份的成員，不僅在就該項決議應否通過的問題上以投票方式表決，會被視為行使該等股份所附有的表決權，而且在就該項決議以投票以外的方式表決，亦被視為行使該等表決權；而且不論公司的章程細-則有任何規定，公司的任何成員，均可要求以投票方式表決該問題。
22	A member who holds shares to which the resolution relates is regarded as exercising the voting rights carried by those shares not only **<u>if</u>** he votes in respect of them on a poll on the question whether the resolution shall be passed, but also **<u>if</u>** he votes on the resolution otherwise than on a poll.	持有與該項決議有關的股份的成員，不僅在就該項決議應否通過的問題上以投票方式表決，會被視為行使該等股份所附有的投票權，而且在就該項決議以投票以外的方式表決，亦被視為行使該等表決權。
23	A relevant shareholder shall be regarded as voting not only **<u>if</u>** he votes on a poll on the question whether the resolution shall be passed, but also **<u>if</u>** he votes on the resolution otherwise than on a poll.	就應否通過該項決議的問題上，有關股東須被視為作出表決一事，不僅在於他有否以投票方式表決，亦在於他有否以投票以外的方式就該項決議作出表決。
24	Subsection (1) shall not be taken as requiring any offer or invitation to be treated as made to the public **<u>if</u>** it can properly be regarded, in all the circumstances, as not being calculated to result, directly or indirectly, in the shares or debentures becoming available for subscription or purchase by persons other than those receiving the offer or invitation.	第(1)款不得視作規定將下述要約或邀請視為向公眾作出，該等要約或邀請為在任何情況下，均可恰當地 被認作並非旨在直接或間接導致股份或債權證可供並非接獲該項要約或邀請的人認購或購買者。

25	This section shall not prevent a subsidiary which is a member of its holding company from accepting and holding further shares in its holding company **if** such further shares are allotted to it as fully paid up in consequence of a capitalization of reserves or profits by such holding company.	本條並不阻止一間作為其控股公司成員的附屬公司，接受及持有更多其控股公司的股份，但該等股份須是該控股公司在將儲備或利潤資本化後，作為全部繳足股款的股份分配予該附屬公司的。
26	The Registrar shall register a prospectus **if** subparagraphs (i), (ii), (iii) and (iv) of paragraph (a) are complied with in respect of that prospectus.	處長須將招股章程註冊，但該招股章程須符合(a)段第(i)、(ii)、(iii)及(iv)節的規定。

To sum up, based on the analysis of various translation methods of the introductory word for conditional clauses 'if,' it is found that methods (I) and (II) translate 'if' as '假若' (jiǎ ruò) or '假使' (jiǎ shǐ); except for two conditional clauses that use the simple present or simple past tense, all the other conditional clauses use the subjunctive mood to express a hypothetical situation that had already occurred in the past or was unlikely to occur in the future. There are also cases using the subjunctive mood to express a hypothetical situation in method (III) in which 'if' is translated as '若' (ruò). In addition, methods (III) and (IV) translate 'if' as '若' (ruò) or '倘' (tǎng)/'倘若' (tǎng ruò), which can be considered synonyms of '如' (rú) and can be used interchangeably to express a conditional situation. That is, if the case mentioned in the conditional clause happens, it will result in the occurrence of the main clause afterwards.

This indicates that in most cases, 89% of the instances of 'if' being translated as '如' (rú), translators consciously or unconsciously follow the consistency principle of legal translation, that is, legal translation is different from the translation of other texts and does not require diverse translation methods. As long as the meaning is consistent with the original text, it is best to maintain the same translation for the same term throughout the whole text, without considering diversified translations.

However, due to the engagement of multiple translators in the translation process of Hong Kong legislation, there may be minor discrepancies in the operative norms of multiple translators in the team work. Different translators have different preferences for word choices, and factors such as considering the Chinese expression habits of the context or avoiding repetition, or the slight negligence of the person responsible for unifying the style of the final translation may result in 'if' being translated as a synonym or near-synonym of '如' (rú) in some cases. That is to say, in the actual operation process, there are still some diverse Chinese translations, and translators do not completely follow the consistency principle of legal translation. Nevertheless, after analysing the different translations mentioned above, using synonyms of '如' (rú) can also achieve the same function as the original text.

Additionally, method (VI) translates 'if' as '在 ...... 情況下' (zài ...... qíng kuàng xià), which refers to the situation in which 'if' introduces two or more conditions. The translation approach is to add such phrases as '在以下情況下/在下述情形下' (zài yǐ xià qíng kuàng xià/zài xià shù qíng xíng xià; in the following cases/under the following circumstances) in the main clause before describing various conditions, so that readers have a rough idea of what will be expressed next. With respect to methods (V), (VI), and (VII), 'if' is respectively translated as '在 ...... 情況下' (zài ...... qíng kuàng xià), '在 ...... 時' (zài ...... shí), or is left untranslated. Based on the new perspective on legal text types proposed in Chapter 3, Hong Kong laws and regulations belong to the vocative text type and function is the most important factor, i.e., the translation should maintain or achieve the same function as the original text. Although these three methods do not fully realise or greatly reduce the meaning of 'if' as a conditional conjunction, they do not affect readers' understanding, especially when other Chinese conjunctions are added to the sentence. Therefore, it can be considered that the same function as the original text has been basically achieved.

In summary, the conditional clauses introduced by 'if' can be divided into three types:

(1) 'If' introduces factual conditional clauses, which can be translated as '若' (ruò), '倘' (tǎng), '倘若' (tǎng ruò), '在 …… 時' (zài …… shí), or left untranslated, in addition to the most common translation '如' (rú).
(2) 'If' introduces non-factual conditional clauses, which use the subjunctive mood to express a higher degree of hypothetical or contradictorysituations, and is translated as '假若' (jiǎ ruò), '若' (ruò), or '假使' (jiǎ shǐ).
(3) 'If' introduces multiple conditional clauses, and is translated as '在 …… 情況下' (zài …… qíng kuàng xià).

4.2.2 Conditional clauses introduced by 'where' and different translations of 'where'

'Where', another common introductory word for conditional clauses, appears 668 times in the whole Companies Ordinance, including the translations shown in Table 4.10.

From Table 4.10, it can be seen that the introductory word 'where' for conditional clauses appears 668 times, of which 331 are translated as '凡' (fán) and 224 are translated as '如' (rú).

There is no big difference between the translation of '如' (rú) and '凡' (fán) for 'where' conditional clauses. But when 'if' is also used in the same sentence, 'where' is translated as '凡' (fán) instead of '如' (rú). Then, under what circumstances is 'where' translated differently? Are there any special purposes for using other translations? Have these different translations achieved the same function as the original text? In this section, different translations of 'where' other than '凡' (fán) and '如' (rú) are analysed in detail.

(I) **'Where' translated as '倘若' (tǎng ruò) and '若' (ruò)**

There are only two sentences in which 'where' is translated as '倘若' (tǎng ruò) and '若' (ruò), as shown in Table 4.11.

Table 4.10 Summary of different translations of 'where' in the Companies Ordinance

Translations of 'where'	*Frequency*	*Percentage*
凡 (fán)	331	50
如 (rú)	224	33
在 …… 情況下 (zài …… qíngvkuàng xià)	13	3
若/倘若 (ruò/tǎng ruò)	2	
在 …… 時/在 …… 後 (zài …… shí/zài …… hòu)	6	
在 …… 地方 (zài …… dì fāng)	87	14

Table 4.11 'Where' translated as '倘若' (tǎng ruò) and '若' (ruò)

No.	*English original*	*Chinese translation*
1	A copy of any trust deed or other document for securing any issue of debentures shall be forwarded to any person requiring it within 20 days of the receipt by the company of the request, on payment in the case of a printed trust deed or other document of the sum of $4 or such less sum as may be prescribed by the company, or **where** the trust deed or other document has not been printed, on payment of $2 for every 100 words or fractional part thereof required to be copied.	任何人如要求取得保證發行債權證的信託契據或其他文件的副本，公司須於接獲該項要求20天內，於收費後將該副本遞送予該人；如屬印製的信託契據或其他文件，所收取的款項為$4或公司所訂明的較少款項，而**倘若**該信託契據或其他文件未經印製，則按所需複制副本的字數計算，每100字(不足100字者亦算作100字)收取$2。
2	Provided that **where** under section 38C the consent of a person is required to the issue of a prospectus and he has given that consent, he shall not by reason of his having given it be liable under this subsection as a person who has authorized the issue of the prospectus except in respect of an untrue statement purporting to be made by him as an expert.	但**若**根據第38C條規定須取得某人的同意始可發出招股章程，而該人已給予該項同意，則該人並不會因給予該項同意而以招股章程的批准發出者身分鬚根據本款負上法律責任，但若該人就一項看來是由其以專家身分作出的不真實陳述而鬚根據本款負上法律責任，則屬例外。

The translation of 'where' as '倘若' (tǎng ruò) and '若' (ruò) only appears twice in the translation of the Companies Ordinance. These two words are synonyms of '如' (rú) and can be used interchangeably, which can achieve the same function as the original text. It is worth noting that the first sentence contains two introductory words for conditional clauses, namely 'in the case' and 'where.' The translation translates 'in the case' as '如' (rú) and 'where' as '倘若' (tǎng ruò) to avoid repetition in Chinese, which is simply because of the expression habits of the Chinese language.

(II) 'Where' translated as '在 …… 時/在 …… 後' (zài …… shí/ zài …… hòu)

There are six sentences in which 'where' is translated as '在 …… 時/在 …… 後' (zài …… shí/zài …… hòu), as shown in Table 4.12.

Table 4.12 'Where' translated as '在 …… 時/在 …… 後' (zài …… shí/zài …… hòu)

No.	*English original*	*Chinese translation*
1	The relevant section is treated as contravened in the case of a distribution unless the statutory requirement about the relevant accounts (that is, the requirement of this section and sections 79G, 79H and 79I, as and **where** applicable) are complied with in relation to that distribution.	在分發中，除非關於有關帳目的法例規定(即本條及第79G、79H或79I條的規定所適用之處及**在**適用的**時候**)已獲遵從，否則視為有關一條的規定被違反。
2	**Where** any such order is made may give such ancillary or consequential directions as it thinks expedient, including a direction that 1 member of the company present in person or by proxy shall be deemed to constitute a meeting.	法院**在**作出任何此等命令**時**，亦可作出其認為合宜的附帶或相應的指示，包括一項公司1名成員親自出席或由代表出席即當作構成一個會議的指示。
3	The settling of lists of contributories and the rectifying of the register of members **where** required, and the collecting and applying of the assets…	議定分擔人列表，**在**有需要**時**將成員登記冊更正，並收集與運用資產……
4	**Where** the lending of money is part of the ordinary business of the company, the lending of money by the company in the ordinary course of its business…	任何公司**在**其通常業務運作**中**藉出款項；而藉出款項為公司通常業務的一部分……
5	**Where** a direction is given under subsection (2) or (4), the Registrar may by a further direction in writing extend the period within which the company is to change its name, at any time before the end of that period.	處長根據第(2)或(4)款發出指示**後**，可隨時在更改公司名稱的期限結束前，以進一步的書面指示將該期限延展。
6	**Where** such a resolution has been passed, an application may be made to the court for the cancellation of the resolution – …	上述決議通過**後**，以下人士可向法院提出取消該決議的申請—……

The translation of 'where' as '在 …… 時' (zài …… shí) appears in three sentences, while the translation of 'where' as '在 …… 後' (zài …… hòu) appears in two sentences. However, upon a closer examination of the original text, it can be seen that 'where' in all the listed instances still functions as an introductory word for conditional clauses. For example, sentence No. 2 can be translated as '**凡**法院作出任何此等命令.' Similarly, sentence No. 5 can also be translated as '處長**如**根據第(2)或(4)款發出指示，則可隨時在更改公司名稱的期限結束前，以進一步的書面指示將該期限延展。' Moreover, it should be noted that 'where' itself does not express the meaning of time or time sequence, so it is more appropriate to translate it as '如' (rú) or '凡' (fán). While '在 …… 時' (zài …… shí) does not express the meaning of 'where' as an introductory word for conditional clauses semantically, it does not affect readers' understanding, and such a translation still basically achieves the same function as the original text.

(III) 'Where' translated as '在 ...... 情況下' (zài ...... qíng kuàng xià)

There are 13 sentences in which 'where' is translated as '在 ...... 情況下' (zài ...... qíng kuàng xià), as shown in Table 4.13.

There are a total of 13 sentences in the Companies Ordinance in which 'where' is translated as '在 ...... 情況下' (zài ...... qíng kuàng xià) or a similar translation. When 'if' introduces two or more conditions, as mentioned in Section 4.2.1, it can be translated as '在 ...... 情況下' (zài ...... qíng kuàng xià). Similarly, there are two occasions when 'where' is translated in this way: (1) when 'where' introduces two or more conditions like 'if' (as in sentences No. 2, 5, 8, 9, and 11), phrases such as '在以下情況下' are used before listing each condition; (2) when 'where' introduces a single condition, it can be translated as '如' (rú) or '凡' (fán), meaning 'if' (as in sentences No. 1, 3, 4, 6, 7, 10, 12, and 13). Although '在 ...... 情況下' (zài ...... qíng kuàng xià) and '如' (rú) or '凡' (fán) have some differences in meaning, they do not affect readers' understanding, so the translation basically achieves the same function as the original text.

(IV) 'Where' translated as '在 ...... 地方' (zài ...... dì fang)

As we know, 'where' is a common introductory word for adverbial clauses of location and is translated as '在 ...... 地方' (zài ...... dì fāng). There are 16 sentences in which 'where' is translated as '在 ...... 地方' (zài ...... dì fāng), which will not be discussed in this study, since this study focuses on the usage of 'where' as an introductory word for conditional clauses.

To sum up, the translation of 'where' in this Companies Ordinance varies. From the above analysis of the translation of 'where' as an introductory word for conditional clauses, we can see that method (I) translates it as '倘若' (tǎng ruò) or '若' (ruò), synonyms of '如' (rú), without affecting the function of the translation. Method (II) translates it as '在 ...... 時/在 ...... 後' (zài ...... shí/zài ...... hòu), indicating the specific time or period related. Method (III) translates it as '在 ...... 情況下' (zài ...... qíng kuàng xià), mainly to introduce multiple conditions, whereas '凡' (fán) can only introduce a single case or occasion that encompasses all situations. Although methods (II) and (III) differ in meaning from the two dominant translation methods '凡' (fán) and '如' (rú), it is acceptable to use these methods considering the multiple conditions in the original text. If '凡' (fán) is used for such multiple conditions, the meaning of the multiple conditions in the original may not be reflected, thus affecting the function of the original text.

4.2.3 Conditional clauses introduced by 'when' and different translations of 'when'

In addition to the two dominant introductory words for conditional clauses 'if' and 'where' in the Companies Ordinance, there are several other introductory words for conditional clauses, including 'when,' 'in (the) case,' and 'in the event.'

Table 4.13 'Where' translated as '在 … 情況下' (zài … qíng kuàng xià)

No.	*English original*	*Chinese translation*
1	At any time after the presentation of a winding-up petition and before a winding-up order has been made, the company or any creditor or contributory may- (a) **where** any action or proceeding against the company is pending in the Court of First Instance or the Court of Appeal, apply to the court in which the action or proceeding is pending for a stay of proceedings therein; (b) **where** any action or proceeding against the company is pending in any court or tribunal other than the Court of First Instance or the Court of Appeal, apply to the Court of First Instance to restrain further proceedings in the action or proceeding, and the court to which application is so made may, as the case may be, stay or restrain the proceedings accordingly on such terms as it thinks fit.	在清盤呈請提出後及在清盤令作出前的任何時候，公司或任何債權人或分擔人— (a) **在**有針對公司的任何訴訟或法律程序在原訟法庭或上訴法庭待決的**情況下**，可向該訴訟或法律程序待決所在的法院申請擱置在該法院進行的法律程序； (b) **在**有針對公司的任何訴訟或法律程序在原訟法庭及上訴法庭以外的任何法院或審裁處待決的**情況下**，可向-原訟法庭申請禁制在該訴訟或法律程序中進行進一步的法律程序， 而有申請如此向某法院提出，該法院可據此而按其認為合適的條款擱置或禁制進行(視屬何情況而定)該等法律程序。
2	**Where** after a company has been dissolved it is proved to the satisfaction of the Registrar- (a) that the company if still existing would be legally or equitably bound to carry out, complete or give effect to some dealing, transaction or matter; and (b) that in order to carry out, complete or give effect thereto, some purely administrative act, not discretionary, should have been done by or on behalf of the company, or should be done by or on behalf of the company if still existing, the Registrar may, as representing the company or its liquidator under this section, do or cause to be done any such act.	在公司解散後，處長如信納**以下情況**已獲證明— (a) 公司如仍存在則會在法律上或衡平法上有責任進行或完成某些交易或事宜或使其生效；及 (b) 為進行或完成該等交易或事宜或使其生效，某些純粹屬行政上而非涉及酌情決定的作為，原應已由公司或代表公司作出，或如公司仍存在則應由公司或代表公司作出，即可根據本條以公司代表或公司清盤人代表的身分，作出或安排作出任何該等作為。

(*Continued*)

Table 4.13 (Continued)

No.	*English original*	*Chinese translation*
3	The Thirteenth Schedule shall apply **<u>where</u>** a company (in that Schedule referred to as the 'repurchasing company') makes a general offer to purchase all of its shares, or all of its shares of a particular class.	附表13適用於**下述情況**：公司(在該附表內稱為"購回公司")作出公開要約以全數購買本身的股份或全數購買本身某個類別的股份。
4	This section and the Ninth Schedule shall apply **<u>where</u>** a company (in this section and the Ninth Schedule referred to as 'the transferee company'), whether a company within the meaning of this Ordinance or not, makes an offer to acquire all the shares, or all the shares of any class or classes, not already held by it in another company (in the Ninth Schedule referred to as 'the transferor company') on terms which are the same in relation to all the shares to which the offer relates or, where those shares include shares of different classes, in relation to all the shares of each class.	本條及附表9適用於**下述情況**：任何公司(在本條中及附表9內稱為"受讓人公司")，不論是否本條例所指的公司，作出一項要約，收購另一間公司(在附表9內稱為"出讓人公司")中其尚未持有的全部股份或任何類別的全部股份，而要約條款就該項要約有關的一切股份而言乃屬相同，或如該等股份包括不同類別的股份，則要約條款就所有屬同一類別的股份而言乃屬相同者。
5	Nothing in subsection (2) shall invalidate the proceedings of a general meeting **<u>where</u>**- (a) …; and (b) …	第(2)款的規定並不**在以下情況下**使某次大會的議事程序失效— (a) ……；而 (b) ……
6	For the avoidance of doubt, it is declared that- (a) the requirement to send a copy of a listed company's relevant financial documents to an entitled person of the company in compliance with section 129G(1) does not apply **<u>where</u>** the company sends a copy of those documents to the person in response to a request under this section; …	為免生疑問，現宣布— (a) 為遵從第129G(1)條而向上市公司的某有權利的人送交該公司的有關財務文件的規定，**在**該公司應本條所指的要求而送交該等文件的**情況下**，並不適用……
7	**<u>Where</u>** that is allowed, 1 or more proxies to attend and vote instead of him, and that a proxy need not also be a member.	**在**容許的**情況下**委任1名或多於1名代表，代其出席會議並表決，以及說明代表本身無須亦為成員。
8	With the exception made by section 48D(6), this section applies **<u>where</u>** the issuing company has secured at least a 90 per cent equity holding in another company in pursuance of an arrangement providing for the allotment of equity shares in the issuing company on terms that the consideration for the shares allotted is to be provided- (a) …; or (b) …	除第48D(6)條所指不適用的個案外，本條於**以下情況**適用：發行公司已依據一項安排取得另一公司最少百分之九十的股份的權益，該項安排規定分配發行公司的權益股份，而分配發行條款是，獲分配的股份的代價須藉下列方式提供— (a) ……；或 (b) ……

9	This section applies **where** the issuing company- (a) …; and (b) …	本條於**以下情況**適用：發行公司— (a) ……；及 (b) ……
10	Subsection (5) shall not apply but the documents referred to in that subsection and, **where** that subsection applies by virtue of subsection (6), the further documents referred to in subsection (6).	第(5)款並不就該項決議而適用，但須時該款提述的文件以及(**在**該款憑藉第(6)款而適用的**情況下**)第(6)款提述的其他文件。
11	With the exception made by section 48D(6), this section applies **where** the issuing company has secured at least a 90 per cent equity holding in another company in pursuance of an arrangement providing for the allotment of equity shares in the issuing company on terms that the consideration for the shares allotted is to be provided- (a) …; or (b) …	除第48D(6)條所指不適用的個案外，本條於**以下情況**適用：發行公司已依據一項安排取得另一公司最少百分之九十的股份的權益，該項安排規定分配發行公司的權益股份，而分配發行條款是，獲分配的股份的代價須藉下列方式提供— (a) ……；或 (b) ……
12	… then- (i) subsection (4) shall not apply but, for the purposes of section 116B(1), a member holding shares to which the resolution relates shall not be regarded as a member who would be entitled to attend and vote; (ii) subsection (5) shall not apply but the documents referred to in that subsection and, **where** that subsection applies by virtue of subsection (6), the further documents referred to in subsection (6), shall be supplied- (A) to each member by whom, or on whose behalf, the resolution is required to be signed in accordance with section 116B; and (B) at or before the time at which the resolution is supplied to the member for signature.	…… 則— (i) 第(4)款並不就該項決議而適用，但就第116B(1)條而言，持有該項決議所關乎的股份的成員不得被視為有權出席和表決的成員； (ii) 第(5)款並不就該項決議而適用，但須時該款提述的文件以及(**在**該款憑藉第(6)款而適用的**情況下**)第(6)款提述的其他文件— (A) 提供予按照第116B條規定須簽署(或由他人代表簽署)該項決議的每名成員；並且 (B) 在提供該項決議予有關成員簽署之時或之前提供予該成員。

(*Continued*)

Table 4.13 (Continued)

No.	*English original*	*Chinese translation*
13	This section and the Ninth Schedule shall apply **where** a company (in this section and the Ninth Schedule referred to as 'the transferee company'), whether a company within the meaning of this Ordinance or not, makes an offer to acquire all the shares, or all the shares of any class or classes, not already held by it in another company (in the Ninth Schedule referred to as 'the transferor company') on terms which are the same in relation to all the shares to which the offer relates or, where those shares include shares of different classes, in relation to all the shares of each class.	本條及附表9適用於**下述情況**：任何公司(在本條中及附表9內稱為"受讓人公司")，不論是否本條例所指的公司，作出一項要約，收購另一間公司(在附表9內稱為"出讓人公司")中其尚未持有的全部股份或任何類別的全部股份，而要約條款就該項要約有關的一切股份而言乃屬相同，或如該等股份包括不同類別的股份，則要約條款就所有屬同一類別的股份而言乃屬相同者。

'When' in the Companies Ordinance has two meanings. First, it expresses its original meaning of 'at the time of,' indicating a temporal subordinate clause relationship. Second, it expresses a condition and is translated as '如' (rú). The second meaning of 'when' as an introductory word for conditional clauses will be discussed in this study. 'When' appears 73 times in the Companies Ordinance, but it is only used as an introductory word for conditional clauses 5 times, all of which are translated as '如' (rú), as shown in Table 4.14. This indicates that 'when' is not a commonly used introductory word for conditional clauses in the Companies Ordinance.

From these five examples, it can be seen that there is no big difference between a conditional clause introduced by 'when' and by 'if.' For example, sentence No. 5 can be expressed as 'if a poll is demanded, regard shall be had to the number of votes to which each member is entitled according to the regulations of the company,' by replacing 'when' with 'if.' Although 'when' appears as a conjunction for conditional clauses in the Companies Ordinance at a very low frequency, translators still need to be careful when translating English legal texts and have to decide the meaning of 'when' in different contexts without treating it directly as its common meaning of 'at the time.'

4.2.4 Conditional clauses introduced by 'in (the) case' and different translations of 'in (the) case'

'In the case' appears 273 times in the Companies Ordinance. The same sampling method mentioned in Section 1.4.3 is employed and a certain number of sentences (i.e., a total of 54 sentences) is selected for analysis. In addition, 'in case' appears 16 times.

There are various translations of 'in the case' in the Companies Ordinance, as shown in Table 4.15.

(I) **'In the case' translated as 如/如屬 (rú/rú shǔ)**

'In the case' is mostly translated as '如/如屬' (rú/rú shǔ; if/if belonging to), 42 times out of 54 sentences. For example: '**In the case**' of refusal of an inspection required under subsection (5) of a directors' statement or auditors' report, the court may by order compel an immediate inspection of that statement or report.' The Chinese translation is '**如屬**有關人士被拒絕根據第(5)款的規定查閱董事陳述書或核數師報告書的情況，法院可藉命令強迫有關公司立即將該陳述書或報告書供有關人士查閱。' 'In the case,' usually translated as '在 …… 情況下' (zài …… qíng kuàng xià), '至於' (zhì yú), or '就 …… 而言' (jiù …… ér yán), does not indicate the meaning of condition. But the meaning of condition is added in the Chinese translation, which is slightly different from its original meaning. However, because such connecting terms as '在 …… 情況下' (zài …… qíng kuàng xià), '至於' (zhì yú), or '就 …… 而言' (jiù …… ér yán) can be omitted in the Chinese

Table 4.14 'When' translated as '如' (rú)

No.	*English original*	*Chinese translation*
1	<u>**When**</u> the Registrar has reasonable cause to believe that a company is keeping a register of members at any place outside Hong Kong without having a valid licence under this Ordinance, he shall publish in the Gazette and send to the company by post a notice that at the expiration of 3 months from the date of that notice the name of the company mentioned therein will, unless cause is shown to the contrary, be struck off the register and the company will be dissolved.	處長**如**有合理因由相信，某公司並無持有根據本條例發給的有效特許證而在香港以外的任何地方備存成員登記冊，則須在憲報刊登公告及將該公告以郵遞方式送交該公司，述明由該公告的日期起計3個月屆滿時，除非該公司提出相反理由，否則該公告內所述公司的名稱即自登記冊中剔除，而該公司亦即解散。
2	A resolution shall be a special resolution <u>**when**</u> it has been passed by not less than three-fourths of the votes cast by such members as, being entitled so to do, vote in person or, where proxies are allowed, by proxy, at a general meeting of which not less than 21 days' notice, specifying the intention to propose the resolution as a special resolution, has been duly given.	**如**某項決議獲表決通過，而所獲得的票數不少於有權在大會上親自表決或委派代表表決(如代表獲准許表決的話)的成員所投票數的四分之三，且已就有關大會妥為發出不少於21天的通知期，指明擬將該項決議列為一項特別決議的意向，則該項決議即為一項特別決議。
3	For the purposes of this section, notice of a meeting shall be deemed to be duly given and the meeting to be duly held <u>**when**</u> the notice is given and the meeting held in manner provided by this Ordinance or the articles.	就本條而言，會議通知書**如**以本條例或章程細則所訂定的方式發出，即須當作妥為發出，而任何會議如以本條例或章程細則所訂定的方式舉行，即須當作妥為舉行。
4	<u>**When**</u> several liquidators are appointed, any power given by this Ordinance may be exercised by such one or more of them as may be determined at the time of their appointment, or, in default of such determination, by any number not less than 2.	**如**有數名清盤人獲委任，本條例所給予的任何權力，可由他們當中一人或多於一人行使，按他們被委任時所決定者而定，或如無上述決定，則可由不少於2的任何數目的清盤人行使。
5	In computing any majority under this section <u>**when**</u> a poll is demanded regard shall be had to the number of votes to which each member is entitled according to the regulations of the company.	**如**有要求以投票方式表決，則在根據本條計算過半數成員人數時，須顧及每名成員按照公司的規例有權投下的票數。

Table 4.15 Summary of different translations of 'in the case' in the Companies Ordinance

Translations	*Frequency*
如/如屬 (rú/rú shǔ)	42
不譯 (no translation)	8
在 …… 情況下/在 …… 中 (zài …… qíng kuàng xià/zài …… zhōng)	3
就 …… 而言 (jiù …… ér yán)	1

expression based on the context, the omission of these words does not affect the function of the translation.

(II) 'In the case' translated as 在 …… 情況下/在 …… 中 (zài …… qíng kuàng xià/zài …… zhōng)

There are three sentences adopting this translation, which maintains the original meaning of 'in the case,' thus keeping the same function as the original text. For example,

> The court may, with a view to bringing to an end the matters complained of, make such other order as it thinks fit, whether for regulating the conduct of the specified corporation's affairs in future, or for the purchase of the shares of any members of the specified corporation by other members of the specified corporation or by the specified corporation and, **in the case** of a purchase by the specified corporation, for the reduction accordingly of the specified corporation's capital, or otherwise.

The Chinese translation is:

> 為了結遭投訴的事項，可作出它認為合適的其他命令，不論是為以下事項或其他事項作出命令：規管日後該指明法團事務的處理方式，或規定該指明法團的其他成員購買該指明法團的任何成員的股份或該指明法團本身購買該指明法團的任何成員的股份以及(**在**由該指明法團本身購買該等股份的**情況下**)該指明法團相應地減少其資本。

'**In the case** of a purchase by the specified corporation' is translated as '**在**由該指明法團本身購買該等股份的**情況下**,' which completely reflects the original meaning of the term and achieves the same function as the original text.

(III) 'In the case' translated as '就 …… 而言' (jiù …… ér yán)

There is only one sentence adopting this translation: 'He shall, **in the case** of the offence mentioned in paragraph (o), be liable to imprisonment, and **in the case** of any other offence shall be liable to imprisonment and a fine.' The Chinese translation is '**就**(o)段所述的罪行**而言**，該人可處以監禁，而就任何其他罪行而言，則可被處監禁及罰款。' 'In the case' in this sentence is translated as '就 ……

而言' (jiù ...... ér yán), which is also the original meaning of the term, thus achieving the same function as the original text.

(IV) 'In the case' with no translation

There are eight sentences with 'in the case' left untranslated. For example,

> The references in subsection (3)(b)(i) to the copy of a contract required thereby to be endorsed on or attached to a copy of the prospectus shall, **in the case** of a contract wholly or partly in a language other than English or Chinese, be taken as references to a copy of a translation of the contract in either language or a copy embodying a translation in English or Chinese of the parts not in either language, as the case may be, being a translation certified in the prescribed manner under subsection (10) to be a correct translation.

The Chinese translation is '凡第(3)(b)(i)款提述招股章程內規定須註明或隨附合約文本之處，而該合約完全或部分既非以中文亦非以英文撰寫，則須視作為提述合約的中文或英文譯本，或提述其內已收錄合約中既非以中文亦非以英文撰寫的部分的中文或英文譯本的合約文本(視屬何情況而定)；而該等譯本均按第(10)款所指的訂明方式核證為正確譯本。' Out of the need for coherence and cohesion in the Chinese language, 'in the case' is left untranslated, but since such connecting terms as '在...... 情況下' (zài ...... qíng kuàng xià), '至於' (zhì yú), or '就 ...... 而言' (jiù ...... ér yán) can be omitted in the Chinese language, the omission of 'in the case' in the Chinese translation here does not affect the function of the translation.

According to *The English-Chinese Word-Ocean Dictionary* (1990: 781), 'in case' and its variants 'in case of' and 'in case that' are the actual introducing words for conditional clauses that express hypothetical relationships, which can generally be translated as '假若' (jiǎ ruò), '如果' (rú guǒ), '假使' (jiǎ shǐ), or '萬一' (wàn yī). However, in the Companies Ordinance, 'in case of' appears only 16 times, of which it is only used in sentences 4 times, as shown in Table 4.16.

'In case of' is translated as '如' (rú) for all four sentences, in which 'default,' 'conflict,' 'difference,' and 'winding up' are the situations introduced respectively. These situations or conditions are all unfavourable or bad conditions of low frequency. Although '如' (rú) encompasses various situations and conditions, '萬一' (wàn yī) or '一旦' (yī dàn) more accurately reflects the meaning of the original text.

It is worth noting that in ordinary English, there is a significant difference between 'in case (of/that)' and 'in the case (of/that),' but in the Companies Ordinance, both in English writing and Chinese translation, the two are not strictly distinguished. The former expresses the meaning of a situation or condition that rarely occurs, while the latter is a general connective phrase that expresses '在 ... 情況下' (zài ...... qíng kuàng xià), '至於' (zhì yú), or '就 ...... 而言' (jiù ...... ér yán), which should be differentiated in writing or translation. For example, 'In case the house burns down, we will get the insurance money.' The Chinese translation is: '萬一房子燒掉，我們會得到保險公司的賠償。' The situation of the

Table 4.16 'In case of' translated as '如' (rú)

No.	*English original*	*Chinese translation*
1	Provided that, **in case of** default in delivering to the Registrar any document within 1 month after the allotment any document required to be delivered by this section, the company, or any person liable for the default, may apply to the court for relief.	但**如**因本條規定須交付的任何文件於作出分配後1個月內仍未交付處長而構成失責，則該公司或任何須對失責負法律責任的人，均可向法院申請寬免。
2	Subject to the provisions of this Ordinance, the liquidator of a company which is being wound up by the court shall, in the administration of the assets of the company and in the distribution thereof among its creditors, have regard to any directions that may be given by resolution of the creditors or contributories at any general meeting, or by the committee of inspection, and any directions given by the creditors or contributories at any general meeting shall **in case of** conflict be deemed to override any directions given by the committee of inspection.	在符合本條例條文的規定下，正在由法院清盤的公司，其清盤人在管理公司資產及將該等資產派發予公司的債權人時，須顧及債權人或分擔人在任何大會上藉決議所給予的任何指示，或審查委員會所給予的任何指示；兩者**如**有衝突，則債權人或分擔人在任何大會上所給予的任何指示，須當作凌駕審查委員會所給予的任何指示。
3	A committee of inspection appointed in pursuance of this Ordinance shall consist of creditors and contributories of the company or persons holding general powers of attorney from creditors or contributories in such proportions as may be agreed on by the meetings of creditors and contributories, or as, **in case of** difference, may be determined by the court.	依據本條例委出的審查委員會，須由公司的債權人及分擔人或持有債權人或分擔人所授予的一般授權書的人，按債權人會議及分擔人會議所協議的比例組成，**如**債權人會議及分擔人會議意見分歧，則按法院裁定的比例組成。
4	**In case of** a voluntary winding up, the company shall, from the commencement of the winding up, cease to carry on its business, except so far as may be required for the beneficial winding up thereof.	**如**屬自動清盤的情況，公司須自清盤開始之時停止營業，但為使公司業務在有利情況下結束而需要繼續營業者除外。

house getting burnt down does not happen frequently, so it is more appropriate to translate 'in case' as '萬一' (wàn yī) or '一旦' (yī dàn). Therefore, legal drafters or translators need to pay attention to the meaning of this phrase, which includes infrequent conditions and cannot simply be regarded as a synonym of 'if.'

4.2.5 Conditional clauses introduced by 'in the event' and different translations of 'in the event'

'In the event' appears 37 times in the Companies Ordinance, with the following several translations, as shown in Table 4.17.

Table 4.17 Summary of different translations of 'in the event' in the Companies Ordinance

Translations	*Frequency*
如 (rú)	20
一旦 (yī dàn)	8
凡 (fán)	1
在 …… 時 (zài …… shí)	7
在 …… 情況下 (zài …… qíngkuàng xià)	1

(I) **'In the event' translated as '如' (rú)**

There are 20 sentences in which 'in the event' is translated as '如' (rú), as shown in Table 4.18.

It is believed that 'in the event' is synonymous with 'if,' 'when,' and 'in case,' but if we carefully observe the conditional sentences introduced by 'in the event,' we find that other introductory words introduce relatively neutral situations, while almost all situations introduced by 'in the event' are negative events that occur infrequently with negative consequences. For instance, situations introduced by sentences No. 1, 6, 7, 9, 10, 11, 13, and 15 are related to the winding up of a company or related fees that need to be paid, etc. Situations introduced by sentences No. 2, 4, 5, 12, and 17 are related to the breach of or non-compliance with regulations or failure to enforce judgements, and so on. Situations introduced by sentences No. 14 and 16 are related to the death or bankruptcy of contributories. Comparatively, situations introduced by sentences No. 3, 8, 18, 19, and 20 are neutral.

Therefore, when translating 'in the event,' although most of the original translations still translate it as '如' (rú), '一旦' (yī dàn) is a better alternative translation that more accurately describes unexpected events that are unlikely to occur or events with negative consequences. Therefore, compared with '如' (rú), '一旦' (yī dàn) is closer to the original meaning of 'in the event.'

Table 4.18 'In the event' translated as '如' (rú)

No.	*English original*	*Chinese translation*
1	**In the event** of the winding up of a company re-registered in pursuance of this section, the following provisions shall have effect- (a) … (b) … (c) …	**如**依據本條重新註冊的公司清盤，以下條文即具效力— (a) …… (b) …… (c) ……
2	**In the event** of non-compliance with or contravention of any of the requirements of this section, a director or other person responsible for the prospectus shall not incur any liability by reason of the non-compliance or contravention, if - (a) … (b) … (c) …	**如**本條任何規定不獲遵從或被違反，董事或其他對招股章程負責的人在下列情況下，不會因有關規定不獲遵從或被違反而招致任何法律責任— (a) …… (b) …… (c) ……
3	Provided that, **in the event** of failure to include in a prospectus a statement with respect to the matters specified in paragraph 19 of Part I of the Third Schedule, no director or other person shall incur any liability in respect of the failure unless it be proved that he had knowledge of the matters not disclosed.	但**如**招股章程內未載有關於附表3第I部第19段指明事項的陳述，則除非能證明有關董事或其他人對未披露的事項知情，否則該人不會因為招股章程內未載有該項陳述而招致任何法律責任。
4	The validity of an allotment shall not be affected by any contravention of the foregoing provisions of this section but, **in the event** of any such contravention, the company and every officer of the company who is in default shall be liable to a fine.	某項分配的有效性，並不因本條中前述的任何條文被違反而受影響；但**如**有任何此等違反條文事，則有關公司及其每名失責高級人員均可處罰款。
5	**In the event** of any default in complying with the provisions of this section, every officer of the company who is in default shall be liable to a fine.	**如**因沒有遵從本條條文而構成失責，公司每名失責高級人員均可處罰款。

(*Continued*)

Table 4.18 (Continued)

No.	*English original*	*Chinese translation*
6	**<u>In the event</u>** of a company being wound up, every present and past member shall be liable to contribute to the assets of the company to an amount sufficient for payment of its debts and liabilities, and the costs, charges, and expenses of the winding up, and for the adjustment of the rights of the contributories among themselves.	**如**公司清盤，每名現在及過去成員均有法律責任分擔提供公司的資產，分擔款額須足夠償付公司的債項及債務，支付清盤的費用、收費及開支，並須足夠作調整分擔人彼此之間的權利之用。
7	The court may, **<u>in the event</u>** of the assets being insufficient to meet the costs, charges and expenses incurred in the winding up, make an order as to the payment thereof out of the assets in such order of priority as the court thinks just.	**如**資產不足夠支付清盤所招致的費用、收費及開支，法院可作出命令，規定該等費用須按法院認為公正的優先次序從資產中撥付。
8	**<u>In the event</u>** of the court ordering the holding of any meetings it may order that the provisions of this Ordinance relating to the holding of meetings be varied, abrogated or added to for the purpose of such meetings.	法法**如**下令舉行任何會議，可下令為舉行該等會議，本條例關於舉行會議的條文，可予更改、撤銷或增補。
9	Subject to section 239A, **<u>in the event</u>** of the winding up continuing for more than 1 year, the liquidator shall summon a general meeting of the company at the end of the first year from the commencement of the winding up, and of each succeeding year, or at the first convenient date within 3 months from the end of the year or such longer period as the Official Receiver may allow, and shall lay before the meeting an account of his acts and dealings and of the conduct of the winding up during the preceding year.	除第239A條另有規定外，**如**清盤持續進行超過1年，清盤人須在清盤開始之時起計第一年終結時，以及在繼後的每一年終結時，或在有關年度終結之時起計3個月內或破產管理署署長所容許的更長時間內的第一個方便日期，召集公司大會，並須將一份關於上一年度其本人的作為及交易以及清盤的進行的報告，在該會議席上提交。
10	**<u>In the event</u>** of the winding up continuing for more than 1 year, the liquidator shall summon a general meeting of the company and a meeting of creditors at the end of the first year from the commencement of the winding up, and of each succeeding year, or at the first convenient date within 3 months from the end of the year or such longer period as the Official Receiver may allow, and shall lay before the meetings an account of his acts and dealings and of the conduct of the winding up during the preceding year.	**如**清盤持續進行超過1年，清盤人須在清盤開始之時起計第一年終結時，以及在繼後的每一年終結時，或在有關年度終結之時起計3個月內或破產管理署署長所容許的更長時間內的第一個方便日期，召集公司大會及債權人會議，並須將一份關於上一年度其本人的作為及交易以及清盤的進行的報告，在該等會議席上提交。

11	**In the event** of a landlord or other person distraining or having distrained on any goods or effects of the company within 3 months next before the date of a winding-up order, the debts to which priority is given by this section shall be a first charge on the goods or effects so distrained on, or the proceeds of the sale thereof.	**如**業主或其他人在緊接清盤令日期前3個月內扣押或曾扣押公司的任何貨品或物品，則獲本條給予優先權的各債項，即為被如此扣押的貨品或物品或出售該等貨品或物品所得收益的第一押記。
12	Provided that execution shall not issue against the effects of any individual member of the company on any judgment, decree, or order obtained in any such action or proceeding, but, **in the event** of the property and effects of the company being insufficient to satisfy the judgment, decree, or order, an order may be obtained for winding up the company.	但不得針對該公司的任何個別成員的財物而提起法律程序，以執行於任何上述訴訟或法律程序中獲得的任何判決、判令或命令，但**如**該公司的財產及財物不足以履行該項判決、判令或命令，則可取得一項將該公司清盤的命令。
13	**In the event** of the company being wound up, every person shall be a contributory, in respect of the debts and liabilities of the company contracted before registration.	**如**該公司清盤，就該公司註冊前所訂約承擔的債項及債務而言，每一人均為分擔人。
14	**In the event** of the company being wound up, every contributory shall be liable to contribute to the assets of the company, in the course of the winding up, all sums due from him in respect of any such liability as aforesaid, and, **in the event** of the death, bankruptcy, or insolvency, of any contributory, the provisions of this Ordinance with respect to the personal representatives and to the trustees of bankrupt or insolvent contributories shall apply.	**如**該公司清盤，在清盤過程中，每名分擔人均負有法律責任向該公司的資產分擔其就前述債務所應付的一切款項；**如**任何分擔人去世、破產或無力償債，則本條例中有關遺產代理人以及破產人的受託人或無力償債分擔人的受託人的條文，即告適用。
15	**In the event** of an unregistered company being wound up, every person shall be deemed to be a contributory who is liable to pay or contribute to the payment of any debt or liability of the company, or to pay or contribute to the payment of any sum for the adjustment of the rights of the members among themselves, or to pay or contribute to the payment of the costs and expenses of winding up the company.	**如**任何非註冊公司清盤，每一人均須當作是分擔人，負有法律責任償付或分擔償付該公司的任何債項或債務，或負有法律責任支付或分擔支付任何款項以調整成員彼此之間的權利，或負有法律責任支付或分擔支付該公司的清盤費用。

(*Continued*)

Table 4.18 (Continued)

No.	*English original*	*Chinese translation*
16	**<u>In the event</u>** of the death, bankruptcy, or insolvency, of any contributory, the provisions of this Ordinance with respect to the personal representatives of deceased contributories and to the trustees of bankrupt or insolvent contributories shall apply.	**如**任何分擔人去世、破產或無力償債，則本條例中有關已故分擔人的遺產代理人以及破產人的受託人或無力償債分擔人的受託人的條文，即告適用。
17	**<u>In the event</u>** of non-compliance with or contravention of any of the requirements imposed by subsection (1)(a) and (b), a director or other person responsible for the prospectus shall not incur any liability by reason of the non-compliance or contravention, if (a) … (b) … (c) …	**如**第(1)(a)及(b)款所訂的任何規定不獲遵從或被違反，董事或其他對招股章程負責的人在下列情況下，不會因有關規定不獲遵從或被違反而招致任何法律責任— (a) …… (b) …… (c) ……
18	Provided that, **<u>in the event</u>** of failure to include in a prospectus a statement with respect to the matters contained in paragraph 19 of the Third Schedule, no director or other person shall incur any liability in respect of the failure unless it be proved that he had knowledge of the matters not disclosed.	但**如**招股章程內未載有關於附表3第19段所載事項的陳述，則除非能證明有關董事或其他人對未披露的事項知情，否則該人不會因為招股章程內未載有該項陳述而招致任何法律責任。
19	**<u>In the event</u>** of the Chief Executive in Council being satisfied that the company is being formed with any such object or for any such purpose, he may order the Registrar to refuse registration of the memorandum and articles, and upon receipt of such order, the Registrar shall, notwithstanding the provisions of section 15, refuse registration of the memorandum and articles.	行政長官會同行政會議**如**信納該公司乃為任何上述目的而組成，可命令處長拒絕將該公司的章程大綱及章程細則註冊，而處長在接獲該命令後，須拒絕將該公司的章程大綱及章程細則註冊，儘管有第15條的規定。
20	**<u>In the event</u>** of the accounts being audited by a public servant there shall be paid to the Government in respect of such audit a sum equal to the fee which would have been chargeable on the audit of the Official Receiver's accounts if the winding up had been a winding up by the court.	**如**帳目由一名公務員審計，則須就上述審計向政府支付一筆款項，數額等於清盤假若是一宗由法院作出的清盤本會就審計破產管理署署長的帳目所徵收的費用。

(II) 'In the event' translated as '一旦' (yī dàn)

There are eight sentences in which 'in the event' is translated as '一旦' (yī dàn), as shown in Table 4.19.

Translating 'in the event' as '一旦' (yī dàn) in these sentences is appropriate and consistent with the context, either expressing the winding up of a company in sentences No. 1, 2, 3, 4, 7, and 8 or expressing the death of a director in sentences No. 5 and 6. Those situations are all infrequent occurrences with a relatively small probability. Therefore, '一旦' (yī dàn) is the most suitable translation, which can accurately convey the same function as the original text. For example, in sentence No. 6, '**in the event** of the death of the director in respect of whom the reserve director is nominated,' the death of a director is an infrequent occurrence. Therefore, translating it as '一旦' (yī dàn) can reflect the low probability of this event happening, and the translation is '某備任董事的提名所關乎的董事**一旦**去世.' However, there are similarities between method (I), which translates 'in the event' as '如' (rú), and method (II), which translates it as '一旦' (yī dàn). 'In the event' in the original English text indicates extremely negative or infrequent situations, which is not differentiated in the Chinese translations of '如' (rú) and '一旦' (yī dàn).

(III) 'In the event' translated as '在 …… 時' (zài …… shí)

There are seven sentences in which 'in the event' is translated as '在 …… 時' (zài …… shí), as shown in Table 4.20.

In these seven sentences, 'in the event' is translated as '在 …… 時' (zài …… shí), but this term does not have the meaning of time but rather indicates a conditional clause that introduces an 'if' condition. Therefore, although the translated meaning is not consistent with the original meaning, the function of the translation is still basically consistent with that of the original text. In addition, these sentences can also be translated as '一旦' (yī dàn) or '萬一' (wàn yī). For example, sentence No. 5 can be translated as '"分擔人" (contributory) 一詞指**一旦**公司清盤，每名有法律責任分擔提供公司資產的人.' Because winding up a company is an unusual event and a critical event for the company itself, the concept of time is relatively unimportant.

(IV) 'In the event' translated as '凡' (fán)

There is only one sentence with 'in the event of' translated as '凡' (fán): 'All moneys and securities paid or delivered into any bank pursuant to this Part **in the event** of a winding up by the court shall be subject in all respects to the orders of the court.' The Chinese translation is '**凡**屬由法院作出的清盤，所有依據本部存入或交付任何銀行的款項及保證物，在各方面均須受法院所作命令的規限。' Considering the subject 'all moneys and securities,' the translation uses '凡' (fán) to be more inclusive, corresponding to 'all' in the original text. The translation of 'in the event' as '凡' (fán) is similar to the original text in terms of function, but it is not a rigorous translation. Using the same phrasal structure ('in the event of a winding up') for the same winding-up case (similar to the previously mentioned

Table 4.19 'In the event' translated as '一旦' (yī dàn)

No.	English original	Chinese translation
1	A company having the liability of its members limited by the memorandum to such amount as the members may respectively thereby undertake to contribute to the assets of the company **in the event** of its being wound up.	公司成員的法律責任，根據章程大綱，限於各成員藉章程大綱承諾在公司**一旦**清盤時所分別分擔提供的公司資產的款額，此等公司在本條例中稱為擔保有限公司。
2	The memorandum of a company limited by guarantee must also state that each member undertakes to contribute to the assets of the company **in the event** of its being wound up while he is a member, or within one year after he ceases to be a member, for payment of the debts and liabilities of the company contracted before he ceases to be a member, and of the costs, charges, and expenses of winding up, and for adjustment of the rights of the contributories among themselves, such amount as may be required, not exceeding a specified amount.	擔保有限公司的章程大綱，亦須述明每名成員承諾於公司在其為成員期間或不再是成員之後一年內**一旦**清盤時，分擔提供不超過指明款額的所需款額予公司的資產，以用於償付公司在其仍為成員期間所訂約承擔的債項或債務，支付清盤的費用、收費和開支，以及用於調整分擔人彼此之間的權利。
3	If the company is to be a company limited by guarantee, the amount that each person who is to be a member is to undertake to contribute to the assets of the company **in the event** of its being wound up…	(如公司將會屬擔保有限公司)每名將會成為成員的人將會承諾在公司**一旦**清盤時，所分擔提供予公司的資產的款額……
4	From the date of incorporation mentioned in the certificate of incorporation, the founder members, together with such other persons as may from time to time become members of the company, shall be a body corporate by the name contained in the memorandum, capable forthwith of exercising all the functions of an incorporated company, and having perpetual succession and a common seal, but with such liability on the part of the members to contribute to the assets of the company **in the event** of its being wound up as is mentioned in this Ordinance.	自公司註冊證書所述的成立日期起，創辦成員連同不時成為公司成員的其他人，即為一個以章程大綱所載名稱為名的法人團體，有能力立即行使一間具法團地位的公司的各項職能，並具有永久延續性及法團印章，而成員的法律責任則一如本條例所述，在公司**一旦**清盤時，需分擔提供公司的資產。
5	Where a private company has only one member and that member is the sole director of the company, the company may in general meeting, notwithstanding anything in its articles, nominate a person (other than a body corporate) who has attained the age of 18 years as a reserve director of the company to act in the place of the sole director **in the event** of his death.	凡某私人公司只有一名成員而該成員是該公司的唯一董事，則不論該公司的章程細則載有任何條文，該公司可在大會上提名一名年滿18歲的人(須不屬法人團體)為該公司的備任董事，**一旦**唯一董事去世，即代替他行事。

6	Subject to compliance with the conditions set out in subsection (9), **<u>in the event</u>** of the death of the director in respect of whom the reserve director is nominated, the reserve director shall be deemed to be a director of the company for all purposes.	在符合第(9)款列明的條件的情況下，某備任董事的提名所關乎的董事**<u>一旦</u>**去世，該備任董事須就所有目的而言當作為該公司的董事。
7	where a company is about to register as a company limited by guarantee, the assent to its being so registered shall be accompanied by a resolution declaring that each member undertakes to contribute to the assets of the company, **<u>in the event</u>** of its being wound up while he is a member, or within 1 year after he ceases to be a member, for payment of the debts and liabilities of the company contracted before he ceased to be a member, and of the costs and expenses of winding up, and for the adjustment of the rights of the contributories among themselves, such amount as may be required, not exceeding a specified amount.	如公司即將註冊為擔保有限公司，成員對公司如此註冊所表示的同意，須附上一項決議，聲明每名成員承諾於公司在其為成員期間或不再是成員之後一年內**<u>一旦</u>**清盤時，分擔提供不超過指明款額的所需款額予公司的資產，以用於償付公司在其仍為成員期間所訂約承擔的債項或債務，支付清盤的費用和開支以及用於調整分擔人彼此之間的權利。
8	The powers of an unlimited company on registration as a limited company to increase the nominal amount of its share capital and to provide that a portion of its share capital shall not be capable of being called up except **<u>in the event</u>** of winding up.	無限公司註冊為有限公司後，在增加其股本的面額以及在訂定其部分股本不能催繳(除於公司**<u>一旦</u>**清盤外)方面的權力。

Table 4.20 'In the event' translated as '在 … 時' (zài … shí)

No.	*English original*	*Chinese translation*
1	A limited company may by special resolution determine that any portion of its share capital which has not been already called up shall not be capable of being called up, except in the event and for the purposes of the company being wound up, and thereupon that portion of its share capital shall not be capable of being called up except **in the event** and for the purposes aforesaid.	有限公司可藉特別決議決定其股本中任何尚未催繳的部分均不能催繳，但公司正**在**清盤或為了配合公司清盤的目的，則屬例外；因此公司該部分的股本，除有前述的情況及為了配合前述的目的外，否則不能催繳。
2	An unlimited company having a share capital may, by its resolution for re-registration as a limited company under section 19, do either or both of the following things, namely- (a) increase the nominal amount of its share capital by increasing the nominal amount of each of its shares, but subject to the condition that no part of the increased capital shall be capable of being called up except **in the event** and for the purposes of the company being wound up; (b) provide that a specified portion of its uncalled share capital shall not be capable of being called up except **in the event** and for the purposes of the company being wound up.	任何有股本的無限公司，可藉公司根據第19條重新註冊為有限公司的有關決議，作出下述兩項或其中一項事情— (a) 增加每股股份的面額，從而增加其股本的面額，但須符合以下條件：除公司正**在**清盤及為了配合公司清盤的目的外，否則所增加的資本完全不能催繳； (b) 訂定公司未催繳股本的其中指明部分，除公司正**在**清盤及為了配合公司清盤的目的外，否則不能催繳。
3	In the case of a company limited by guarantee, no contribution shall, subject to the provisions of subsection (3), be required from any member exceeding the amount undertaken to be contributed by him to the assets of the company **in the event** of its being wound up.	如屬擔保有限公司，在不抵觸第(3)款的條文下，成員無須作出超過其承諾**在**公司清盤**時**會分擔提供作為公司資產的款額的分擔。
4	In the winding up of a company limited by guarantee which has a share capital, every member of the company shall be liable, in addition to the amount undertaken to be contributed by him to the assets of the company **in the event** of its being wound up, to contribute to the extent of any sums unpaid on any shares held by him.	在有股本的擔保有限公司清盤時，公司的每名成員除有法律責任分擔提供其所承諾**在**公司清盤**時**會分擔提供作為公司資產的款額外，尚有法律責任就其所持有的任何股份的任何未繳款額作出分擔。

5	The term 'contributory' (分担人) means every person liable to contribute to the assets of a company **<u>in the event</u>** of its being wound up, and for the purposes of all proceedings for determining, and all proceedings prior to the final determination of, the persons who are to be deemed contributories, includes any person alleged to be a contributory.	'分擔人'(contributory) 一詞指每名**在**公司清盤**時**有法律責任分擔提供公司資產的人，而就所有為裁定何人須當作為分擔人而進行的法律程序，及所有在最終裁定前進行的法律程序而言，亦包括任何被指稱為分擔人的人。
6	Such sum is, under the contract or in the ordinary course of business, payable in a place outside Hong Kong where assets of the company are maintained and under the law of that place the claim in respect of which the sum is payable is, **<u>in the event</u>** of a winding up, accorded priority with respect to those assets over claims which under the contract or in the ordinary course of business are payable at any other place…	根據該份合約或在通常業務運作中，該筆款項須在公司保有其資產的香港以外地方支付，而根據該地方的法律，**在**清盤之**時**，就該等資產而言，導致該筆款項須予支付的申索，相對於根據該份合約或在通常業務運作中須在任何其他地方支付的申索，是具有優先權的……
7	Provided that an unregistered company shall not, except **<u>in the event</u>** of its being wound up, be deemed to be a company under this Ordinance, and then only to the extent provided by this Part.	但非註冊公司除**於**清盤**時**，不得當作為本條例所訂的公司，而當作為本條例所訂的公司時，亦只限於本部所訂定的範圍。

translations), '一旦' (yī dàn) or '萬一' (wàn yī) would be more appropriate, because a winding-up order issued by the court is case-specific and a critical contingency for the company itself, rather than a typical and frequent event. Therefore, translating 'in the event of' as '一旦' (yī dàn) is a more appropriate translation that accurately conveys the original meaning and achieves the same function as the original text.

(V) 'In the event' translated as '在 …… 情況下' (zài …… qíng kuàng xià)

There is only one sentence with 'in the event' translated as '在 …… 情況下' (zài …… qíngkuàng xià):

> Any conveyance, mortgage, delivery of goods, payment, execution or other act relating to property made or done by or against a company within 6 months before the commencement of its winding up which, had it been made or done by or against an individual within 6 months before the presentation of a bankruptcy petition on which he is adjudged bankrupt, would be deemed in his bankruptcy a fraudulent preference, shall **in the event** of the company being wound up be deemed a fraudulent preference of its creditors and be invalid accordingly.

The Chinese translation is:

> 在公司清盤開始前6個月內，由公司作出或針對公司作出的任何轉易、按揭、貨品交付、付款、簽立或其他與財產有關的作為，假若是在某個別人士被判定破產的破產呈請提出前6個月內，由該名人士作出或針對該名人士作出，本會在其破產案中被當作為一項欺詐優惠者，則**在**公司清盤的**情況下**，須當作為一項給予公司債權人的欺詐優惠，並須據此而無效。

'In the event' as the introductory word for conditional clauses is not translated, which can be translated as '則一旦公司清盤,' as a company being wound up is not a frequent occurrence. The translation of '在 …… 情況下' (zài …… qíngkuàng xià) merely basically reflects the original meaning and achieves the same function as the original text.

To sum up, 'in the event' is translated in five ways, among which method (IV), the translation of '凡' (fán), and method (V), the translation of '在 …… 情況下' (zài … qíng kuàng xià), have a low proportion and can be considered exceptional cases. Method (III), the translation of '在 …… 時' (zài …… shí), can be regarded as expressing a condition that is currently happening and can achieve the same function as the original text. Therefore, it can be accepted as a reasonable translation. In spite of a higher proportion of the translation '如' (rú) in method (I), '一旦' (yī dàn) is the most appropriate translation on the basis of examining the conditions introduced by 'in the event' in the original text. Although the translation '如' (rú) does not affect the function of the translation, '一旦' (yī dàn) is the most suitable and recommended translation for 'in the event' in the Companies Ordinance, considering the original meaning and the context in which it is usually used.

4.2.6 Conditional clauses introduced by 'providing/provided' and different translations of 'providing/provided'

There are three meanings of 'provided' in the Companies Ordinance:

(I) 'Provided', the passive voice of the verb 'provide,' means 'regulating.' For example,

> For the purposes of this section, notice of a meeting shall be deemed to be duly given and the meeting to be duly held when the notice is given and the meeting held in manner **provided** by this Ordinance or the articles.

The Chinese translation is:

> 就本條而言，會議通知書如以本條例或章程細則所訂定的方式發出，即須當作妥為發出，而任何會議如以本條例或章程細則所訂定的方式舉行，即須當作妥為舉行。

(II) 'Provided' as the passive voice of the verb 'provide' means 'offering or giving.' For example,

> In the case of a listed company, section 47C(4) authorizes the giving of financial assistance only if the company has net assets which are not thereby reduced or, to the extent that those assets are thereby reduced, if the assistance is **provided** out of distributable profits.

The Chinese translation is:

> 就上市公司而言，只有在淨資產不會因給予資助而減少的情況下，或如淨資產會因此而減少，亦只有在引致資產減少的資助是從可分發利潤中獲得提供的情況下，第47C(4)條始許可給予資助。

'The assistance is provided' means 'the assistance is offered or given.'

(III) 'Provided' means a 'proviso.' For example, '**Provided** that before a licence is so revoked, the Registrar shall give to the body notice in writing of his intention, and shall afford it an opportunity of being heard in opposition to the revocation.' Its Chinese translation is '但處長在如此撤銷特許證前，須向該團體發出書面通知，說明其意圖，並須給予該團體就反對該項撤銷而陳詞的機會。' 'Provided that' is translated as '但' (dàn), a proviso expressing concession. It is a relatively fixed expression in legal English. This usage is common in the Companies Ordinance.

Surprisingly, the term 'provided that' is not used in the whole Companies Ordinance as a condition. Moreover, a similar term, 'providing that,' is also absent from the Ordinance. Another similar term 'provide for' means 'to establish provisions for' or 'to make provisions for,' which however does not convey the meaning of a condition. This finding contradicts the common view that 'provided/providing that' is used to express a condition. This at least indicates that 'provided/providing that' is not a commonly used conditional phrase in the Companies Ordinance.

4.2.7 Conditional clauses introduced by 'should' and different translations of 'should'

'Should' appears 39 times in the Companies Ordinance, and is translated as '應' (yīng), '應該' (yīng gāi), '應當' (yīng dāng), or '将' (jiāng; will). For example,

> If the Official Receiver is of the opinion that the remuneration of a liquidator as determined under subsection (2)(a) **<u>should</u>** be reviewed the Official Receiver may apply to the court, and the court may make an order confirming, increasing or reducing the remuneration of the liquidator.

The Chinese translation is:

> 如破產管理署署長認為根據第(2)(a)款釐定的清盤人酬金**應**予檢討，破產管理署署長可向法院申請，而法院可作出命令，以確認、增加或削減清盤人的酬金。

'Should' is translated as '應' (yīng). Another similar example:

> Where the petition is presented by members of the company as contributories on the ground that it is just and equitable that the company **<u>should</u>** be wound up, the court shall not refuse to make a winding-up order on the ground only that some other remedy is available to the petitioners unless it is also of opinion that they are acting unreasonably in seeking to have the company wound up instead of pursuing that other remedy.

The Chinese translation is:

> 呈請是由公司成員以分擔人身分提出，其理由是將公司清盤是公正公平的，法院不得僅以呈請人尚有其他補救方法而拒絕作出清盤令，但如法院同時認為呈請人尋求**將**公司清盤而不採用該其他補救方法屬不合理，則屬例外。

'Should' is translated as '将' (jiāng), which expresses the future tense.

Therefore, the term 'should' used in the whole Companies Ordinance does not convey the meaning of a condition, indicating that 'should' is not a commonly used conditional phrase in the Companies Ordinance without the meaning of 'if.' However, the use of 'should' as an introductory word for conditional clauses is more common in business contracts, as it is often necessary to express hypothetical situations (such as force majeure) in contracts. By contrast, using 'should' to express such unlikely hypothetical situations in laws and regulations is extremely rare.

4.3 Summary

In this chapter, several introductory words for conditional clauses, including 'if,' 'where,' 'when,' 'in the event,' and 'in (the) case,' are firstly analysed in the Companies Ordinance to examine their different translations and whether these translations accurately and fully convey the original meaning and achieve the same function as the original text. Although there are various translations for different introductory words for conditional clauses, some common translations are easily spotted, including '如' (rú), '凡' (fán), '在 …… 情況下' (zài …… qíng kuàng xià), '在 …… 時' (zài …… shí), and omission. Although these translations may not fully convey the meaning or significantly reduce the meaning as a condition, they do not affect readers' understanding of the text as a whole. Therefore, the translation basically achieves the same function as the original text. Additionally, '倘' (tǎng) and '若' (ruò) are synonyms of '如' (rú), so these translations also achieve the same function as the original text. This shows that the Chinese translation of the Companies Ordinance does not strictly follow the consistency principle of literal translation, with minor adjustments made in specific contexts.

The usage and translation of each of these introductory words for conditional clauses are summarised below:

(1) 'If' is used to introduce three types of conditional clauses. The first type is introducing a factual conditional clause in the present tense or present perfect tense, 89% of the instances of which are translated as '如' (rú), and occasionally as '倘/倘若' (tǎng/tǎng ruò), '在 ...... 時' (zài ...... shí), or omitted. The second type is introducing a non-factual conditional clause, i.e., the subjunctive mood for expressing hypothetical situations or situations contrary to facts, which is translated as '假若/若/假使' (jiǎ ruò/ruò/jiǎ shǐ). The third type is introducing multiple conditional clauses, which is translated as '在 ...... 情況下' (zài ...... qíngkuàng xià).
(2) Fifty per cent of the conditional clauses introduced by 'where' are translated as '凡' (fán). There are differences between 'if' and 'where' in both writing and translation. In writing, 'if' usually introduces a less important condition, while 'where' introduces a broader and more important case. In translation, 'if' is translated as '如' (rú) while 'where' is usually translated as '凡' (fán).
(3) 'When' is used to introduce conditional clauses only five times in the Companies Ordinance. The Chinese translation is '如' (rú), which is consistent with the commonly used translation of 'if'—'如' (rú). This indicates that there is not much difference between 'when' and 'if' when they are used to introduce conditional clauses.
(4) 'In case' and 'in the case' are not differentiated in writing and translation in the Companies Ordinance. The former is used to indicate an unlikely event or a rare situation, while the latter is a general conjunction expressing the meaning of '在 ...... 情況下' (zài ...... qíng kuàng xià), '就 ...... 而言' (jiù ...... ér yán), or '至於' (zhìyú). It is important to note the difference between the two in legal writing and legal translation.
(5) 'In the event' is used to introduce events that are rare and often negative, such as company liquidation, breach of provisions, death of directors, bankruptcy, or insolvency. Although the majority of instances are translated as '如' (rú), '一旦' (yī dàn) and '萬一' (wàn yī) are better alternatives to describe unexpected or disastrous events.
(6) 'Providing/provided that' and 'should' are not used as introductory words for conditional clauses in the Companies Ordinance. 'Providing/provided that' is only used in the form of proviso, while 'should' is only used in its common English usage of '應' (yīng; should) and '應該' (yīng gāi; should).

Although efforts have been made to compare and differentiate the usage and translation of these introductory words for conditional clauses, it is found that English

Table 4.21 Different translations for different introductory words for 'company liquidation'

1	**If** the winding up had been a winding up by the court 假若是一宗由法院作出的清盤
2	**In the case of** a winding up 在該宗清盤中
3	General Power of Court **in case of** Winding Up by Court 在由法院作出清盤的情況下法院所具的一般權力
4	**In the event of** the winding up of a company re-registered in pursuance of this section如依據本條重新註冊的公司清盤
5	**In the event of** winding up (公司)一旦清盤
6	**In the event of** a winding up 在清盤之時
7	**In the event of** a winding up by the court 凡屬由法院作出的清盤

writing and Chinese translation often use these introductory words interchangeably. For example, the original English text often uses different introductory words to refer to the situation of 'company liquidation,' such as 'in the event,' 'if,' 'in the case,' and 'in case,' and the Chinese translation does not seem to distinguish these introductory words, as shown in Table 4.21.

Although legal writers do not strictly differentiate these introductory words for conditional clauses and use them relatively freely in the drafting process, and translators do not necessarily distinguish among them, it is still possible to identify dominant translations for these introductory words and spot differences among them.

References

Barber, C.L. Some measurable characteristics of modern scientific prose. In *Contributions to English Syntax and Phonology*. Stockholm, 1962.

Bhatia, Vijay K. *Analysing Genre—Language Use in Professional Settings*. New York: Longman Group Limited, 1993.

Coode, George. *On Legislative Expression; or, The Language of the Written Law*. Introduction to a digest of the Poor Laws attached to the 1843 Report of the Poor Law Commission. Repr. In Drieger, E.A. (1957), The Composition of Legislation, 1848.

Chao, Yuen Ren. *A Grammar of Spoken Chinese*. Berkeley; Los Angeles: University of California Press, 1968.

Jiang, Yan [蔣嚴]. 漢語條件句的違實解釋 [On the counterfactual reading of Chinese conditionals]. In 語法研究和探索 [*Studies and Investigations on Chinese Grammar*] 北京：商務印書館 [Beijing: The Commercial Press], 2000: 257–279.

Li, Kexing [李克興]. 法律英語條件句的寫作和翻譯 [Composing and translating conditional clauses in legal texts]. 中國翻譯 [*Chinese Translators Journal*], 2008 (4)：71–77, 96.

Lu, Gusun [陸谷孫]. 英漢大詞典（第2版）[*English-Chinese Dictionary* (second edition)]. 上海：上海譯文出版社 [Shanghai: Shanghai Translation Publishing House], 2007.

Wang, Tongyi (ed.) [王同億(主編譯)]. 英漢辭海 [*The English-Chinese Word-ocean Dictionary*]. 北京：國防工業出版社 [Beijing: National Defense Industry Press], 1990.

Xu, Yangchun [徐陽春]. 現代漢語複句的各種類型 [*A Study on Sentence Patterns of Modern Chinese Complex Sentences*]. 北京：中國社會科學出版社 [Beijing: China Social Sciences Press], 2002.

現代漢語辭海 [*Modern Chinese Word-Ocean Dictionary*]. 新华出版社 [Xinhua Publishing House], 2002.

Online Oxford English Dictionary: https://www.oed.com

5 Translation patterns and analytical methods of conditional clauses

5.1 Translation patterns of conditional clauses introduced by 'if'

This section, by analysing the examples extracted by the sampling method mentioned in Section 1.4.3, mainly explores the translation patterns of conditional clauses introduced by 'if.'

(I) 'If' is used before the main clause, and the Chinese translation is '如' (rú), which is also put before the main clause. It can be generalised as: 'if' conditional clause + main clause ➔ '如' (rú) conditional clause + main clause. There are a total of 176 sentences extracted, of which 124 sentences are translated using the first translation pattern, accounting for 70% of the total. It can be seen that this translation pattern is the most common one in the Companies Ordinance.

For example,

English original: **If** any prospectus is issued in contravention of this section the company and every person who is knowingly a party to the issue thereof shall be liable to a fine.

Chinese translation: **如**招股章程違反本條而發出，則有關公司及每名明知自己是發出招股章程其中一方的人，均可處罰款。

(II) 'If' is used after the main clause, and the Chinese translation is '如' (rú), which is put before the main clause. It can be generalised as: main clause + 'if' conditional clause ➔ '如' (rú) conditional clause + main clause. There are 28 sentences using the second translation pattern, accounting for 16%.

For example,

English original: For the purposes of this subsection, a sum shall be deemed to have been paid to and received by the company **if** a cheque for that sum has been received in good faith by the company and the directors of the company have no reason for suspecting that the cheque will not be paid.

Chinese translation: 就本款而言，**如**該公司已真誠收到繳付該款項的支票，而該公司的董事並無理由懷疑該支票會不獲兌現，則該筆款項須當作已付予該公司及已由該公司收到。

DOI: 10.4324/9781003359180-5

This is because there is no fixed requirement in English for the position of conditional clauses, which can be placed in the middle, beginning, or end of a sentence. However, in Chinese expressions, the conditional clause is generally stated before the main clause, that is, the Chinese language tends to first explain the hypothetical situation, and then describe what will happen under the hypothetical situation. This is why the dominant structure for expressing conditions in Chinese is usually '如果 …… 那麼' (rú guǒ …… nà me) or '如 …… 則' (rú …… zé). However conditional clauses in Chinese can also be placed after the main clause, but this is generally done for a special meaning, such as to emphasise a certain element.

(III) 'If' is used after the main clause, and the Chinese translation is '如' (rú), which is also put after the main clause. It can be generalised as: main clause + 'if' conditional clause ➔ main clause + '如' (rú) conditional clause. There are only two sentences translated in this way.

Example 1:

English original: A special resolution passed by a company is not effective for purposes of section 47E-

(a) unless the statement required by section 47E(6) is available for inspection by members of the company at the meeting at which the resolution is passed;

(b) if it is cancelled by the court on an application under this section.

Chinese translation: 就第47E條而言，公司所通過的特別決議並無效力—

(a) 但如在通過該決議的大會上，備有第47E(6)條所規定的陳述書，供與會的公司成員查閱者則除外；

(b) 如法院應根據本條提出的申請將該特別決議取消。

Example 2:

English original: A member of the committee may be removed by an ordinary resolution at a meeting of creditors, if he represents creditors, or of contributories, if he represents contributories, of which 7 days' notice has been given, stating the object of the meeting.

Chinese translation: 該委員會的任何委員，可在任何債權人會議上(如其代表債權人)或在任何分擔人會議上(如其代表分擔人)，被與會人士藉普通決議將其免任，但有關該會議的通知書必須已於該會議日期的7天前發出，並須述明會議的目的。

As shown in Example 1, the main clause is followed by two situations (a) and (b), with (b) being a conditional clause introduced by 'if.' But due to the structural constraints of the digital table format in legal translation, the translation should try to maintain the same consistent structure as the original text as far as possible. Although in Chinese syntax, the conditional clause tends to be placed before the main clause, this sentence structure will not cause ambiguity.

As for Example 2, although the Chinese translation of the 'if' clause is placed after the main clause, parentheses are added as a supplementary element, which does not affect the overall sentence structure.

(IV) 'If' is put in the middle of the main clause, and the Chinese translation is '如' (rú), which is also put in the middle of the main clause. There are seven sentences following the fourth pattern. Two examples are used for elaboration.

Example 1:

English original: In exercising, as regards any purpose of this Ordinance, the power conferred on him by subsection (1), the Registrar may, **if he thinks fit**, specify 2 or more different forms to be used in respect of that purpose, in different circumstances.

Chinese translation: 處長就本條例的任何目的行使其獲第(1)款授予的權力時，**如他認為合適**，可指明2款或多於2款的不同格式，以供在不同的情況下就該目的而使用。

Example 2:

English original: A limited company, **if so authorized by its articles**, may, by special resolution, alter its memorandum so as to render unlimited the liability of its directors, or managers, or of any managing director.

Chinese translation: 任何有限公司**如獲其章程細則許可**，可藉特別決議修改其章程大綱，使其董事、經理或任何董事總經理的法律責任成為無限的。

The conditional clauses introduced by 'if' are put in the middle of the main clauses: either being put after modal verbs such as 'may' or 'shall' (as shown in Example 1), or being put after the subject (as shown in Example 2). In these cases, the structure of the conditional clause is relatively simple and short, and can be regarded as a supplementary element or an inserted element. The Chinese translation also follows the same pattern, with conditional clauses introduced by '如' (rú) being put in the middle of the main clauses.

In summary, although 'if' conditional clauses include four patterns, the common patterns are only the first two: (I) and (II). That is to say, the main translation patterns of 'if' conditional clauses can be summarised into two types: 'if' clause + main clause (in English) → '如' (rú) clause + main clause (in Chinese); main clause + 'if' clause (in English) → '如' (rú) clause + main clause (in Chinese). Regardless of the position of 'if' before or after the main clause, when translating into Chinese, translators usually put the 'if' conditional clause before the main clause. If this pattern can be understood, translators can grasp the dominant translation pattern when encountering 'if' conditional clauses in the process of translating legal texts.

5.2 Translation patterns of conditional clauses introduced by 'where'

This section, by analysing the examples extracted by the sampling method mentioned in Section 1.4.3, mainly explores the translation patterns of conditional clauses introduced by 'where.' There are a total of 133 sentences extracted, which have the following translation patterns.

(I) 'Where' is used before the main clause, and the Chinese translation is '凡' (fán), which is also put before the main clause. It can be generalised as: 'where' conditional clause + main clause ➔ '凡' (fán) conditional clause + main clause. Among the 133 sentences extracted, 57 sentences use the first translation pattern, accounting for 43% of the total, indicating that this translation pattern is quite common in the Companies Ordinance.

For example,

English original: **Where** the proposed reduction of share capital involves either diminution of liability in respect of unpaid share capital or the payment to any shareholder of any paid-up share capital, and in any other case if the court so directs, the following provisions shall have effect, subject nevertheless to subsection (3).

Chinese translation: 凡建議的股本減少涉及減輕未繳款股本的法律責任，或涉及付款予任何持有繳足款股本的股東，或如在其它情況下法院如此指示，則除第(3)款另有規定外，下述條文具有效力。

(II) 'Where' is used before the main clause, and the Chinese translation is '如' (rú), which is also put before the main clause. It can be generalised as: 'where' conditional clause + main clause ➔ '如' (rú) conditional clause + main clause. Among the 133 sentences extracted, 29 sentences use the second translation pattern, accounting for 22% of the total, which is the second most common translation pattern in the Companies Ordinance.

For example,

English original: **Where** that company is a subsidiary and both a majority of its directors and a majority of the directors of any of its holding companies made such a statement, the date on which the earliest of the statements was made.

Chinese translation: 如公司是一間附屬公司，而其過半數董事以及其任何控股公司的過半數董事均作出上述陳述書，則為作出最早一項陳述書的日期。

(III) 'Where' is used after the main clause, and the Chinese translation is '凡' (fán), which is put before the main clause. There is only one sentence using this pattern.

For example,

English original: Section 64 shall apply **where** a company's articles are by virtue of subsection (1) deemed to contain a provision for the variation of the rights attached to a class of shares as it applies where the articles in fact contain such a provision.

Chinese translation: <u>凡</u>一間公司的章程細則憑藉第(1)款而當作載有一項關於更改附於某一類別股份的權利的條文，第64條即屬適用，猶如該條適用於章程細則事實上載有該項條文一樣。

As mentioned earlier, because the Chinese language tends to express the conditional clause before the main clause, the translation of this sentence is more consistent with the Chinese expressions.

(IV) 'Where' is used after the main clause, and the Chinese translation is '如' (rú), which is put before the main clause. There are two sentences following this pattern, which is similar to the third pattern, with the conditional clause being put before the main clause in the translation.

For example,

English original: For the purposes of this section, 'court' (法院) includes a magistrate <u>**where**</u> the application under this section is made in the course of a prosecution in which the person is adjudged guilty of a default referred to in subsection (1) and, as a result, subsection (2) applies to him.

Chinese translation: 就本條而言，如本條所訂的申請是在該人被判定犯了第(1)款所提述的失責罪的檢控過程中提出的，以致第(2)款適用於該人，則'法院'(court) 包括裁判官。

(V) 'Where' is put in the middle of the main clause, and the Chinese translation is '凡' (fán), which is put before the main clause. There are two sentences following this pattern, similar to the third and fourth patterns, with the conditional clause being put before the main clause in the translation.

For example,

English original: Every statement in lieu of prospectus delivered under subsection (1) shall, <u>**where**</u> the persons making any report required by Part II of the Second Schedule have made therein or have, without giving the reasons, indicated therein any such adjustments as are mentioned in paragraph 5 of the Second Schedule, have endorsed thereon or attached thereto a written statement signed by those persons setting out the adjustments and giving the reasons therefor.

Chinese translation: <u>凡</u>作出附表2第II部所規定的報告的人已在報告內作出，或在並無提出有關理由的情況下，已在報告內表明任何附表2第5段所述的調整，則每份根據第(1)款交付的代替招股章程陳述書，均須註明或附有列明該等調整及就調整提出理由的書面陳述，並由該等人士簽署。

(VI) 'Where' is put in the middle of the main clause, and the Chinese translation is '如' (rú), which is put before the main clause. There is only one sentence following this pattern.

For example,

English original: The expenses of and incidental to an investigation by an inspector appointed by the Financial Secretary under section 142 or 143 shall be defrayed in the first instance out of the general revenue of Hong Kong, but the following persons shall, to the extent mentioned, be liable to repay such expenses to the Government-

(a) …;

(b) …;

(c) any body corporate dealt with by the report, **where** the inspector was appointed otherwise than of the Financial Secretary's own motion, shall be liable, except so far as the Financial Secretary otherwise directs; and

(d) …;

and any amount for which a body corporate is liable by virtue of paragraph (b) shall be a first charge on the sums or property mentioned in that paragraph.

Chinese translation: 財政司司長根據第142或143條委任審查員進行一項調查所需及附帶的費用，須由香港政府一般收入中先行撥款支付，但以下的人須在所述的範圍內，負上向政府償還該等費用的法律責任—

(a) ……；

(b) ……；

(c) 上述報告所處理的法人團體 (如該審查員並非由財政司司長主動委任)須負法律責任，但如財政司司長另作指示則除外；及

(d) ……，

此外，法人團體憑藉(b)段而負上法律責任的任何款額，須為該段中所述款項或財產的第一押記。

In this example, the conditional clause introduced by 'where' is enclosed in parentheses in the Chinese translation, the same as in the original text, and is translated as an inserted element.

In the last four cases (III), (IV), (V), and (VI), although it is not common to have 'where' in the middle or at the end of the sentence, the Chinese translations are very similar, expressing the conditional clause before the main clause. Therefore, regardless of the position of 'where,' at the beginning, in the middle, or at the end of the sentence, the conditional clause introduced by the Chinese translations '凡' (fán) or '如' (rú) always appears before the main clause.

In summary, although the conditional clauses introduced by 'where' include six patterns, only the first two patterns are common. Therefore, the main translation patterns of 'where' conditional clauses can be summarised as two types: 'where' clause + main clause ➔ '凡' (fán) clause + main clause; 'where' clause + main clause ➔ '如' (rú) clause + main clause. These two translation patterns account for 43% and 22% of the 133 sentences respectively. In other words, 'where' usually appears at the beginning of the sentence, and in this case, it is translated as '凡' (fán) or '如' (rú), and the word order is consistent with the original text. If this can be fully understood, translators can grasp the basic translation pattern when translating 'where' conditional clauses in legal texts. Although 'where' is mostly translated as '凡' (fán) and '如' (rú), the dominant translation for 'where' is '凡' (fán) based on the proportion. Even if it is translated as '如' (rú), it can still be replaced by '凡' (fán) without affecting the meaning or function.

5.3 Analytical methods of conditional clauses introduced by 'where' and 'if'

In this section, different methods of decomposing and analysing conditional clauses (especially introduced by 'if' and 'where') are presented. On the one hand, it is helpful to understand the differences between 'if' and 'where' conditional clauses in terms of writing and translation; on the other hand, it is useful to apply different analytical methods for long, complicated conditional clauses in legal texts. As mentioned in Section 4.1.3, the usage of 'where' and 'if' is different and the sequence cannot be reversed when they occur in the same sentence. Then how about their translation? Does the translation follow the original sequence?

One example from the Companies Ordinance (i.e., example 3 in Section 4.1.3) is used to illustrate how different methods are used to analyse sentence structures and explore translations of the introductory words 'where' and 'if.'

> English original: Where the Official Receiver becomes the liquidator of a company, whether provisionally or otherwise, he may, if satisfied that the nature of the estate or business of the company, or the interests of the creditors or contributories generally, or there are other grounds therefor, require the appointment of a special manager of the estate or business of the company other than himself, apply to the court, and the court may on such application, appoint a special manager of the said estate or business to act during such time as the court may direct, with such powers, including any of the powers of a receiver or manager, as may be entrusted to him by the court.

5.3.1 Method of chunking

There are usually three steps involved.

Step 1: looking for clue words, such as 'and,' 'or,' 'provided that' (a common term for introducing a proviso), 'unless,' 'to the extent of,' 'until,' 'where,' or 'if,' so as to chunk long sentences into smaller segments. Obviously, in this sentence, we have three clue words 'where,' 'if,' and 'and,' which are helpful for us to chunk the long sentence into four segments.

- Segment 1 of legal case: Where the Official Receiver becomes the liquidator of a company, whether provisionally or otherwise,

- Segment 2 of legal condition: if satisfied that the nature of the estate or business of the company, or the interests of the creditors or contributories generally, or there are other grounds therefor, require the appointment of a special manager of the estate or business of the company other than himself,
- Segment 3 of main clause 1 (legal subject + legal action): he may apply to the court,
- Segment 4 of main clause 2 (legal subject + legal action): the court may on such application, appoint a special manager of the said estate or business to act during such time as the court may direct, with such powers, including any of the powers of a receiver or manager, as may be entrusted to him by the court.

Step 2: translating each part separately: note tricky words such as 'otherwise,' archaic words such as 'therefor,' and proper terms such as 'Official Receiver.'

- Segment 1: 凡破產管理署署長成為公司的清盤人，不論是臨時或屬其它情況，
- Segment2:如信納基於公司的產業或業務性質，或基於債權人或分擔人的一般利益，或基於其它理由，需要在其本人以外另委一名公司產業或業務的特別經理人，
- Segment 3: 他可向法院申請，
- Segment 4: 法院可應該申請而委任一名上述產業或業務的特別經理人，在法院所指示的期間內行事，該經理人並具有法院所託付的各項權力，其中包括接管人或經理人所具有的任何權力。

Step 3: polishing and finalising the translation: try to make the sentence readable and coherent with some necessary adjustments.

凡破產管理署署長成為公司的清盤人，不論是臨時或屬其它情況，如其信納基於公司的產業或業務性質，或基於債權人或分擔人的一般利益，或基於其它理由，需要在其本人以外另委一名公司產業或業務的特別經理人，則可向法院申請，而法院可應該申請而委任一名上述產業或業務的特別經理人，在法院所指示的期間內行事，該經理人並具有法院所託付的各項權力，其中包括接管人或經理人所具有的任何權力。

5.3.2 Method of tabulating

Similar to the method of chunking, the method of tabulating also involves three steps.

Step 1: tabulating the long sentence in the form of a table: the main clauses in the left column and the subordinate clauses in the right column, as shown in Table 5.1.

Step 2: translating each tabulated part separately, as shown in Table 5.2.

Step 3: polishing and finalising the translation.

凡破產管理署署長成為公司的清盤人，不論是臨時或屬其它情況，如其信納基於公司的產業或業務性質，或基於債權人或分擔人的一

般利益，或基於其它理由，需要在其本人以外另委一名公司產業或業務的特別經理人，則可向法院申請，而法院可應該申請而委任一名上述產業或業務的特別經理人，在法院所指示的期間內行事，該經理人並具有法院所託付的各項權力，其中包括接管人或經理人所具有的任何權力。

Table 5.1 Method of tabulating—Original English

	Where the Official Receiver becomes the liquidator of a company, whether provisionally or otherwise, if satisfied that the nature of the estate or business of the company, or the interests of thc creditors or contributories generally, or there are other grounds therefor, require the appointment of a special manager of the estate or business of the company other than himself,
he may apply to the court, and the court may on such application, appoint a special manager of the said estate or business to act during such time as the court may direct, with such powers, including any of the powers of a receiver or manager, as may be entrusted to him by the court.	

Table 5.2 Method of tabulating—Chinese translation

	凡破產管理署署長成為公司的清盤人， 不論是臨時或屬其它情況， 如其信納基於公司的產業或業務性質， 或基於債權人或分擔人的一般利益， 或基於其它理由，需要在其本人以外 另委一名公司產業或業務的特別經理人，
he may apply to the court, and the court may on such application, appoint a special manager of the said estate or business to act during such time as the court may direct, with such powers, including any of the powers of a receiver or manager, as may be entrusted to him by the court.	可向法院申請， 法院可應該申請而委任一名上述產業或業務 的特別經理人，在法院所指示的期間內行 事，該經理人並具有法院所託付的各項權 力，其中包括接管人或經理人所具有的任 何權力。

5.3.3 Method of diagramming

Similar to the methods of chunking and tabulating, the method of diagramming also involves three steps.

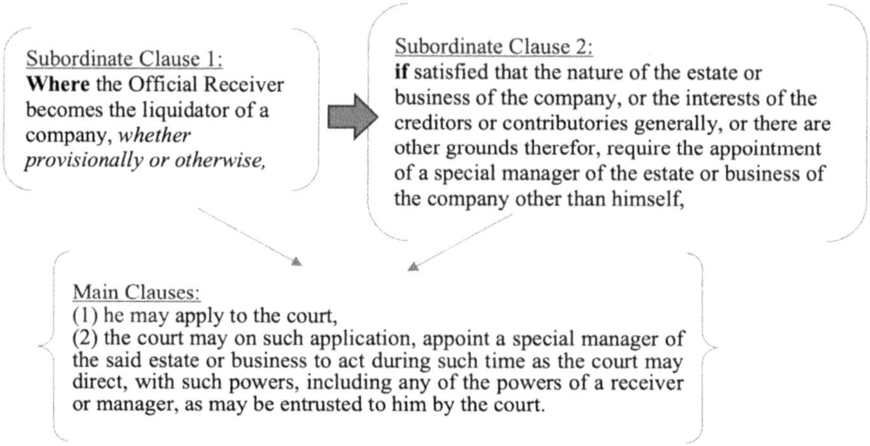

Figure 5.1 Method of diagramming—English original.

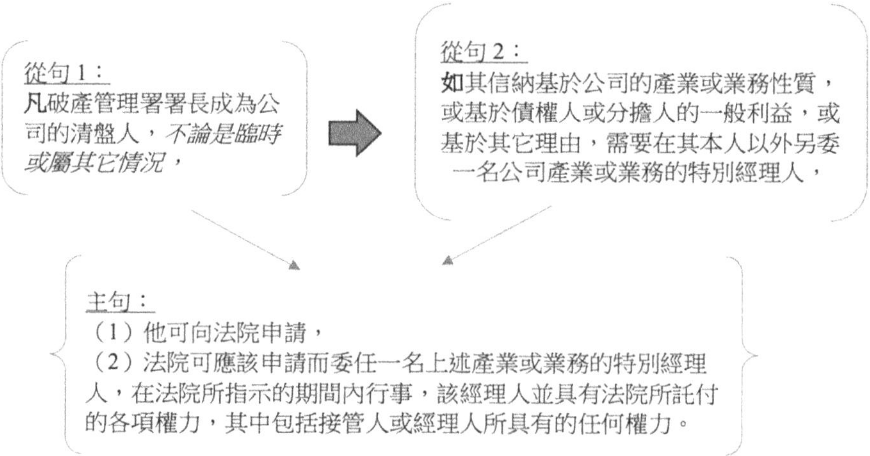

Figure 5.2 Method of diagramming—Chinese translation.

Step 1: diagramming the relationship between different parts of the long sentence for readers to have a clear picture of the relations, as shown in Figure 5.1.
Step 2: translating each part accordingly, as shown in Figure 5.2.
Step 3: polishing and finalising the translation.

凡破產管理署署長成為公司的清盤人，不論是臨時或屬其它情況，如其信納基於公司的產業或業務性質，或基於債權人或分擔人的一般利益，或基於其它理由，需要在其本人以外另委一名公司產業或業務的特別經理人，則可向法院申請，而法院可應該申請而委任一名上述產業或業務的特別經理人，在法院所指示的期間內行事，該經理人並具有法院所託付的各項權力，其中包括接管人或經理人所具有的任何權力。

The essence of these three methods is decomposing the logical relations between each chunk of the original long sentence before translation. If the long sentence is decomposed into several shorter chunks, readers or translators will find it easy to understand or translate. One-paragraph-one-sentence structure intimidates a good number of translators, but if this structure can be chopped up into shorter clauses, it is far easier to cope with. Based on the analysis of the example, it is also clear to readers the differences between 'if' and 'where' when they are used in the same sentence. 'Where' conditional clauses must be put before 'if' conditional clauses, and 'if' conditional clauses cannot be put before 'where' conditional clauses. Besides the sequence, the difference is also related to their usage: 'where' is used to introduce a general legal case of broader scope while 'if' is used to introduce a specific legal condition of narrower scope. Therefore, the translation of these two introductory words is also different when they are used together: 'where' is translated as '凡' (fán), echoing its meaning of compassing everything, and 'if' is translated as '如' (rú), reflecting its meaning of introducing a hypothetical condition.

5.4 Summary

This chapter focuses on the conditional clauses introduced by 'if' and 'where' in the Companies Ordinance and identifies the following translation patterns. There are two main types of conditional clauses introduced by 'if': 'if' clause + main clause (in English) ➔ '如' (rú) clause + main clause (in Chinese), and main clause + 'if' clause (in English) ➔ '如' (rú) clause + main clause (in Chinese). There are also two main types of conditional clauses introduced by 'where': 'where' clause + main clause (in English) ➔ '凡' (fán) clause + main clause (in Chinese), and 'where' clause + main clause (in English) ➔ '如' (rú) clause + main clause (in Chinese). In other words, regardless of the position of 'if' and 'where' in the sentence, the conditional clause is usually placed at the beginning of the translation, which is consistent with Chinese expression habits. This is because the main clause is the core content of the sentence (i.e., end focus), and the subordinate clause is usually placed at the beginning of the sentence in Chinese. This also includes placing the subject of the main clause before the subordinate clause. Therefore, when translating this type of conditional clause, translators should remember this translation technique, that is, the conditional clause in English can be placed before or after the main clause, but in Chinese, the conditional clause is mostly placed before the main clause. Based on the summarised sentence structures of conditional clauses, it is hoped that translators would refer to the summarised sentence structures in translating conditional clauses, so as to ensure the consistency of the translation and more accurately reflect the author's intention in using the same terms in the original text.

In addition, translators find it difficult to decompose long sentences, so three common analytical methods are introduced in Section 5.3. These three methods are useful for readers and translators in understanding the logic and inherent relations in long sentences. The differences are clear between the two introductory words 'where' and 'if' and their varying translations. Though 'where' can be translated as '如' (rú), when it is used together with 'if' in one legal sentence, 'where' is usually translated as '凡' (fán).

6 Conclusion

6.1 Research findings

This book, adopting a descriptive research method, analyses the translation of the Companies Ordinance in Hong Kong, particularly the translation of clauses containing adverbial clauses of condition. Although there have been scholars who have analysed legal texts from the perspective of conditional clauses, there are few studies focusing on specific texts based on corpus research. The research findings of this book on translation theory and translation practice are as follows.

Firstly, in terms of theoretical research, the author reviewed and summarised the theory of translation typology and found that different scholars have varying opinions on the types of legal texts. Based on this, the author proposed a new viewpoint on the types of legal texts. When the function of the translated text is consistent with that of the original text, the function of the legal text is vocative. When the function of the translated text is inconsistent with that of the original text, the function of the original text is vocative, and the function of the translated text can be informative or expressive. As the bilingual ordinances in Hong Kong have equal legal effect, the function of the translated text is consistent with that of the original text, and therefore, the bilingual ordinances in Hong Kong should be considered as vocative texts. In vocative texts, the function or intention is the most important factor.

Secondly, in terms of practical research, based on the above-mentioned viewpoint on the types of legal texts, this study conducted a specific analysis of different translations of introductory words for conditional clauses in the Companies Ordinance to examine whether the different translations achieve the same function as the original text. The research findings on translation practice mainly focus on the translation of conditional sentences in legal texts, which can be summarised below:

(1) The importance of conditional clauses: although some scholars have discussed the importance of conditional clauses before, their discussions were mostly based on subjective impressions from reading English legal texts. This study conducted a statistical analysis based on the thickest law in Hong Kong, the Companies Ordinance, to comprehensively understand the importance of conditional clauses. Although the statistical method used in this study is simple, it

DOI: 10.4324/9781003359180-6

provides readers with a comprehensive understanding of conditional clauses. Out of the 2,247 sentences in the entire Companies Ordinance (marked by a full stop), there are 987 conditional sentences, accounting for 44% of all sentences. It can be sufficiently stated that conditional clauses are the dominant sentence structure in legal texts, and the study of conditional sentences is of great significance from both the legal writing and translation perspectives.

(2) Conditional clauses dominantly introduced by 'if' and 'where': in the Companies Ordinance, conditional sentences introduced by 'if' and 'where' appear 872 and 668 times respectively (calculated by the frequency of appearance of the introductory words), accounting for 45% and 34% of all introductory words for conditional clauses respectively. Conditional clauses introduced by the secondary introductory words 'in (the) case,' 'in the event,' and 'when' are much less frequent, accounting for only 21% of all introductory words for conditional clauses.

(3) Translations for main introductory words for conditional clauses
   (a) There are multiple Chinese translations for the introductory words for conditional clauses 'if' and 'where,' such as '如' (rú), '倘若' (tǎng ruò), '假使' (jiǎ shǐ), and '凡' (fán).
   (b) Other secondary translations include '倘' (tǎng), '若' (ruò), '在 ...... 情況下' (zài ...... qíng kuàng xià), '在 ...... 時' (zài ...... shí), or no translation. It can be seen that, in actual legal writing and translation, writers and translators do not always strictly follow the principle of consistency between legal writing and translation. They may use synonyms or near-synonyms for a particular word, depending on the specific context. Regarding translation, there is more diversity in translation methods, which means that the objectively described results are somewhat different from the prescriptive translation methods. However, overall, the translators of the Companies Ordinance still follow the consistency principle of translation.
   (c) It is worth noting that when 'if' introduces a non-factual conditional clause, meaning a hypothetical or contrary-to-fact situation, and the subjunctive mood is used, indicating a higher degree of hypotheticality, or a situation contrary to fact, it is translated as '假若' (jiǎ ruò), '若' (ruò), or '假使' (jiǎ shǐ) which reflects that translators have noticed the difference between these translations and '如' (rú).

(4) The translation of other introductory words for conditional clauses: in addition to the previous analysis of the translation of 'if' and 'where' in the Companies Ordinance, this study differs from Li's (2008: 71–77) views on the introductory words for conditional clauses in legal texts. The findings are summarised below:
   (a) 'Should' does not indicate '如' (rú) but appears as its original meaning of '應' (yīng) or '應該' (yīng gāi).
   (b) 'Providing/provided that' both appear in the form of proviso and do not indicate the meaning of '如' (rú).
   (c) 'When' appears as an introductory word for conditional clauses only five times, all translated as '如' (rú), indicating that 'when' is not a commonly

used introductory word for conditional clauses in the Companies Ordinance.

(d) Most of the situations introduced by 'in the event' are rare and negative. Therefore, '一旦' (yī dàn) or '萬一' (wàn yī) is a better alternative translation to describe unexpected or catastrophic events.

(e) 'In case (of/that)' and 'in the case (of/that)' are quite different, but in the Companies Ordinance, neither English writing nor Chinese translation strictly distinguish between the two. The former indicates hypothetical or rarely occurring circumstances and is generally translated as '如果' (rú guǒ), '假使' (jiǎ shǐ), or '萬一' (wàn yī) while the latter is a general conjunction indicating '在 …… 情況下' (zài …… qíng kuàng xià), '就 …… 而言' (jiù …… ér yán), or '至於' (zhì yú). Therefore, in writing and translation, the two should be differentiated. The four sentences in the Companies Ordinance using 'in case' all introduce rare or negative situations. Although it is translated as '如' (rú), '一旦' (yī dàn) or '萬一' (wàn yī) is a more appropriate translation based on the original meaning.

(5) The dominant translation patterns of conditional clause structures: based on the specific analysis of the Companies Ordinance, there are two dominant translation patterns for conditional sentences introduced by 'if':

(a) 'If' clause + main clause ➔ '如' (rú) clause + main clause.

(b) Main clause + 'if' clause ➔ '如' (rú) clause + main clause.

For conditional sentences introduced by 'where,' there are also two dominant translation patterns:

(a) 'Where' clause + main clause ➔ '凡' (fán) clause + main clause.

(b) 'Where' clause + main clause ➔ '如' (rú) clause + main clause.

(6) The difference between introductory words for conditional clauses 'if' and 'where' and their implications for translators:

(a) There are differences in the use of 'if' and 'where' in writing and translation. In writing, 'if' expresses a simple condition and usually introduces a less important condition, while 'where' refers to all situations within a certain scope and introduces more important cases. When the two appear in the same sentence, there are obvious differences in terms of sequence and importance. In translation, 'if' is translated as '如' (rú), while 'where' is usually translated as '凡' (fán). Although Coode (1848) initially proposed that there were differences in the usage of 'if' and 'where,' the findings in this study have strengthened and confirmed this viewpoint from a quantitative perspective.

(b) Although there are differences between 'if' and 'where' as conjunctions of conditional clauses, the differences between several other conjunctions are not significant. For example, 'when' and 'if' can often be used interchangeably in English and translated as '如' (rú) in Chinese, and 'in (the) case' is not significantly different from 'if' and can be translated similarly as '如' (rú) or '在 …… 情況下' (zài …… qíng kuàng xià).

(c) Compared with situations introduced by 'if,' 'when,' and 'in (the) case,' which are generally neutral events, most situations introduced by 'in the event' are bad events with negative consequences.
(d) Although the analysis of the text of the Companies Ordinance reveals some differences between the use of conjunctions of conditional clauses, the use of these conjunctions is often somewhat arbitrary. Nonetheless, it can still be seen that 'if' is translated as '如' (rú) in most cases, 'where' is translated as '凡' (fán) in most cases, and 'when' and 'in (the) case' are both translated as '如' (rú).

(7) The impact of different translations of introductory words for conditional clauses on the functional equivalence of the translation: although the main conditional sentence conjunctions 'if,' 'where,' 'when,' 'in (the) case,' and 'in the event' have different translations, the different translations do not significantly affect readers' understanding of the overall content of the original text. Therefore, the translated text generally achieves the same function or conveys the same intention as the original text. 'If,' 'when,' and 'in (the) case' are generally neutral events, and 'in the event' introduces relatively negative events. Although different translations of introductory words for conditional clauses do not significantly affect or basically do not affect the functional equivalence of the translation, synonyms such as '倘' (tǎng) and '若' (ruò) can be used interchangeably with '如' (rú). Therefore, the translation achieves the same function as the original text. In other words, since different translations of introductory words for conditional clauses do not significantly affect or basically do not affect the functional equivalence of the translation, different translations can be used in the process of translating legal texts. However, it is suggested that the translation should follow the original content and style and use the same term for the translation of specific words without using near-synonyms, in order to follow the principle of consistency in translating legal sentence structures and the translation of specialised terminology. It is unnecessary to use different translations for the same term in the original text, such as translating 'if' as '如' (rú) and 'where' as '凡' (fán) in the translation of Hong Kong ordinances. Additionally, even if the original text uses multiple conjunctions such as 'if,' 'when,' and 'in (the) case' to express conditions, the same translation can be used in the translation if there is no special intention or expression of special meaning.

(8) Analytical methods for long legal sentences: to better understand the differences between 'if' and 'where,' one example in which the two words are used in the same sentence is used. In the example, when three analytical methods are introduced to decompose a long legal sentence and analyse relations between different chunks, their different usage and translation are clear: 'where' is translated as '凡' (fán), echoing its meaning of compassing everything, and 'if' is translated as '如' (rú), reflecting its meaning of introducing a hypothetical condition. The three methods are also useful for those who are afraid of long complicated legal sentences.

6.2 Research prospect

The findings of this study, such as the statistical analysis of introductory words for conditional clauses in the Companies Ordinance and the examination and analysis of the data, are helpful for legal English writing and legal teaching. They provide a systematic and clear understanding of how to use and translate introductory words for conditional clauses for legal writers and translators, especially for students studying legal translation. For example, the summarised translation patterns for 'if' and 'where' conditional clauses can help translators effectively translate conditional clauses and distinguish between the two, providing references for legal writers and translators. Additionally, the analysis and comparison of several introductory words for conditional clauses and their translations reveal the frequency of use and commonly used translations, which can provide translation references for translators when they translate conditional clauses.

Despite the research findings and achievements presented in this study, there are still limitations. A detailed analysis of the conditional clauses in the Companies Ordinance was conducted, but due to the limited length, not every conditional clause was covered, and a sampling method was used. This study found that some introductory words for conditional clauses are not strictly distinguished in writing or translation. Given that conditional clauses are the most important sentence structure in legal texts, the author suggests that further in-depth analysis and research should be conducted in the future. It is recommended that future researchers expand the scope of the study to include other categories of legal texts to discover whether other legal texts also make strict distinctions between these introductory words for conditional clauses. Additionally, the translation patterns for conditional clauses presented in this study need to be verified and improved by legal translators in their translation process.

Index

For Product Safety Concerns and Information please contact our EU representative GPSR@taylorandfrancis.com
Taylor & Francis Verlag GmbH, Kaufingerstraße 24, 80331 München, Germany

www.ingramcontent.com/pod-product-compliance
Ingram Content Group UK Ltd.
Pitfield, Milton Keynes, MK11 3LW, UK
UKHW021027180425
457613UK00021B/1097
9781032416694